IMPACT@WORK
Volume 1
Self-Awareness
Behavior &
Motivation

Speaking of impact:

If you think you're too small to have an impact, try going to bed with a mosquito

Anita Roddick, Founder, The Body Shop

Know thyself

Timeless Ancient Greek Wisdom

From disucssion with readers:

'It's when things are tough that we may really stand out'

'...but first, understand what you're up against – then, get out of your own way'

Bobby Mehdwan

Bobby's had a 25-year career in blue-chip corporate management, coaching individuals and implementing change projects in perhaps a hundred companies in several industries all over the world.

He's seen the best of the best do what they are excellent at on countless production floors, office floors, in office networks and in boardrooms. In the process, he's won and lost many corporate battles and learnt many strategies on exactly what creates impact in the workplace.

Around the middle of his career, Bobby decided to make *impact* a big part of his personal development, wanting to know if there was a way to codify and replicate what the best of the best do naturally in order to elevate impact. Over the years, he found snippets and bit-parts of disconnected learning, but couldn't find a single place where it all came together. So, he made it his challenge to piece together one simple, all-encompassing system for everything he needed to know.

Through observation, systematic learning and practice, and by teaching others he's pulled together impact strategies you can use to significant effect.

Bobby's also a Master of Science and Bachelor of Engineering.

Cover by one designs

Published by 60 Strategies Ltd

Copyright 2016 Bobby Mehdwan. All Rights Reserved. You may not copy, store, distribute or transmit any part of this book by any means—except for brief quotations in reviews—without prior written permission from the publisher.

You may also be interested in the Impact@Work podcast via iTunes or RSS

Find out more about other titles, coaching, training or speaking at 60strategies.com.

Connect

@bobbymehdwan   uk.linkedin.com/in/bobbymehdwan   facebook.com/60strategies

Contents

Introduction and About the Series 1

So, What is Impact? 4

Four Components of Impact 5

How to Start 9

Themes 13

Connecting: Self-awareness Behavior & Motivation 15

    Strategy #1: Choose an Optimal Mode of Operation 22

    Strategy #2: Your Inner Parent, Adult and Child 36

    Strategy #3: I'm Okay? Are You Okay? 47

    Strategy #4: The Right Relationships are Everything 51

    Strategy #5: What Motivates You? What Do You Really Value? 61

    Strategy #6: What Drives You? 69

    Strategy #7: Are Limiting Beliefs in Your Way? 73

    Strategy #8: Driving with the Brakes On 79

    Strategy #9: Sprinkle on Some Gestalt 89

    Strategy #10: Ladder of Inference (or Judgment) 94

    Strategy #11: Step Outside Your Comfort Zone – About 4% Out Should Do It – and Get Creative 103

    Strategy #12: Avoid What You're Not Cut Out For. 108

    Strategy #13: Work Somewhere You Like 111

    Strategy #14: *The Force* Won't Help You 113

    Strategy #15: Get a Coach or a Mentor 116

Strategy #16: Anxiety Attack! 119

Strategy #17: Manage Expectations and Don't Be High Maintenance 125

Closing Remarks 128

Introduction and About the Series

Let's start with an idea – is there anyone out there who doesn't want to make a big impact? Anyone at all?

I think it's fair to assume we all want to make an impact. In fact, we intuitively understand that it's something we all need in order to get ahead.

You probably know and want to emulate people with impact. You may describe them as having a natural flair, which seems to confer them an unfair advantage – unfair in the sense that we've introduced something that's about more than how hard they work, or how good they are at what they do. People with impact overcome obstacles with ease, and engage others with grace, exerting influence on everything around them.

But their advantage seems as intangible as charisma.

Now, let's switch to – perhaps – your side of the table.

However hard you work, it can seem like others around you make a bigger impact *and* make it look easy. You have difficult interactions at work where you just can't get through to the people who are important to you – you see things one way and they see it another. You may have felt disadvantaged at some point in your career, as if you just didn't cut it, and the feeling may have lingered like a chip on the shoulder – even if, on paper, you had the best accolades for your job. Others, with flair got promoted quicker, leaving you – working hard! You didn't enjoy or get the most out of what you were doing.

It's easy to label this as a confidence problem or consign it to feelings of inferiority in highly competitive workplaces. But if that is the case, what should you do?

Understand that there is limited value in simply trading self-work for recognition in the workplace. Churning out hard work is a hygiene factor (an expected minimum) in the most demanding of workplaces.

Learning to navigate the politics of an organization and understand how people work are more rewarding than *hard* work for more *hard* work.

Supremely impactful people practice impact strategies and thrive.

Impact means you're not just doing your own thing (which is easy), but doing it *with others,* which is much, much harder.

You can only stand out when you master working with others. But first, you have to master being worked with – making it productive and worthwhile for others to work with you. That comes from knowing yourself so you can put your best foot forward.

Mastering interactions may also be the key to enjoying your work. When you reflect, you may discover that you enjoyed, most, the work you did with people who clicked. The opposite is probably just as true.

Knowing yourself isn't the same thing as specialized technical knowledge about your chosen field. That's clearly essential to function effectively and fulfill your role – just as medics must know medicine and managers must know their business. Marketers won't get far without commerciality and so on. But what makes one marketer more impactful than another? Why do some managers make it up the pole faster, all other things being equal? It's not just their technical knowledge, but how they deploy themselves – in a deeply personal sense.

The big challenge for most of us is underinvesting in impact skills while favoring technical skills which look good on a resume. Those however are easily replicated and often abundant. They may confer diminished competitive advantage alone. Furthermore, in many industries, technical knowledge is merely a resource or perhaps a political currency if you know how to acquire and deploy it well where others are involved.

Nevertheless, from this point on, we'll assume that you have the requisite technical skill, capability or knowledge for your role, because without that, little in this series will elevate you further.

So, What is Impact?

When most people think about impact, they visualize another person dressed to kill, communicating smoothly and powerfully, exuding magnetism and invisibly influencing others around them. Everyone's mesmerized, they turn to jellies and eventually melt into puddles!

Okay, so while the last part's a bit far-fetched, ultimately yes, this sounds like impact. However, this is projection (or delivery) impact and that's just one element of the whole package. Here's the thing – impact sits on top of a solid foundation. Without a foundation it's just fluff and blows around in the wind like in a cardboard TV character.

However, impact is also hard to describe. So, how can we tie it down?

Four Components of Impact

What is it that impactful people do? Are they born naturals?

That's certainly what I've always believed. And perhaps the answer is yes, by virtue of personality. But, it's almost certain that everything they know was learnt at some point, whether or not they were consciously aware of it – or even care to admit it.

If you practice impact, however, you'll be in rarified company that's difficult for rivals to replicate.

Technical skills and knowledge aside, some traits shared by impactful people are:

1. High levels of self-awareness and an ability to negotiate through challenging circumstances
2. An ability to focus on areas of strength utilizing tailored systems and processes to achieve goals
3. Confidence to project powerfully and influence others for the best outcomes
4. Highly strategic, competing vigorously when required and able to ward off rivals effortlessly.

Let's take a more detailed look at this book: Volume 1: *Connecting: Self-awareness Behavior & Motivation.*

Highly self-aware people connect with themselves and others in a unique and powerful way. They:

- Know what they want with clarity. Others around them know it clearly too, but they negotiate so everyone feels like they've won
- Understand how they themselves operate and how others around them operate too, to facilitate cooperation
- Use heightened self-awareness to get out of their own way and to avoid tripping themselves up when things get difficult, deploying deliberate mental strategies to overcome their own – very human – in built limitations
- Choose how to react and behave in their best interests in all situations. They say no when something's not working and work where they're at their best
- Use their knowledge to get the best out of others too.

Most of us lack self-awareness and go through life inadvertently tripping ourselves up when things get difficult, without ever realizing it. We simply don't know when we're shooting ourselves in the foot.

We exit the stage before we – or others – can make a positive impact. But by learning self-awareness you're learning the essentials of presence, which opens the door for big impact.

So, in this series you'll first understand how you and others tick, how to use that to your advantage and then get out of your own way. You'll understand how others may help or hinder you.

Getting others to act for you is the very foundation of impact, so it's essential to understand what moves people – including you – and how your behavior elicits or hinders action.

You can think of Volume 1 as strategies to facilitate a **meeting of minds**.

In Volume 2: *Doing: Achieve Notable Goals* you'll learn to do what you do best and do it the best you can. We'll look at turning your motivations into notable goals, so you can create unbeatable substance with solid foundations.

Volume 3 will then show you the secrets of *Projecting: Communicate & Lead with Power & Presence*. You will learn to lead and face the world in a compelling way by telling good stories which get others on-side. We'll dissect leadership, story-telling and negotiation.

Finally, in Volume 4: *Competing: Secure your Limelight* we'll look at how to stack systems in your favor and prevent others encroaching and stealing your limelight. You'll learn how to leapfrog and carefully manage out rivals looking for a share of the spoils.

That's impact!

Four Components of Impact

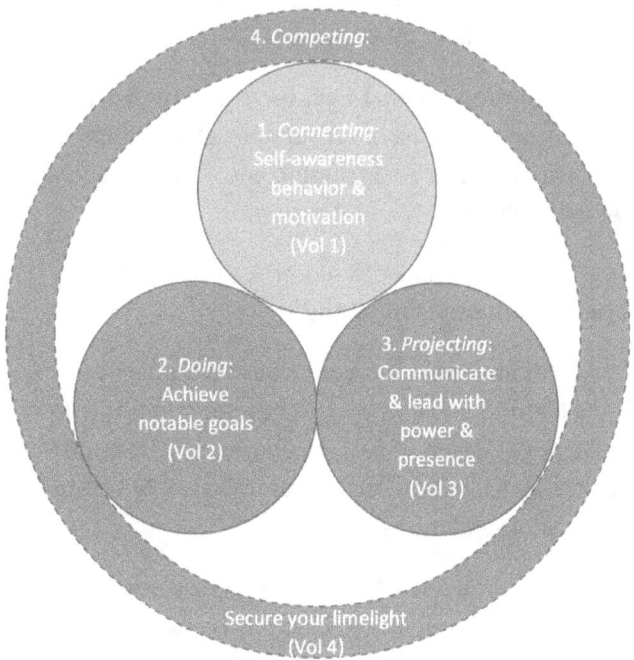

But wait a moment! You're up against a lot here!

Impact is clearly a skill set in its own right, just like knowing how to play an instrument, or code a program or develop products. When practiced over a lifetime, it will push and keep you streets ahead of the pack.

Without any of these strategies under your belt, you're going to work every day without speaking the language of elites. If you think simply turning up, or doing what you do best, or training to improve skills, or putting in the hours, or doing what your boss wants, is enough to make a big impact, you're probably in for a big surprise. No matter what your capability or competence at your job, you *will be* limited and manipulated by others who know how to make a bigger personal impact. With most or all of the following strategies in your toolkit, you will be a powerhouse in virtually any organization or marketplace.

If you think that you're not in this game yet you are going to work with other people, you *are* in this game. You're being played without accepting it.

How to Start

Several people I have coached over the years have said: *If only I knew this when I started...*

I couldn't agree more. In a sense, the series is written for my – relatively naïve – twenty something self, starting the world of work, clutching degree certificates and feeling like they meant everything.

Have you ever thought: *Wouldn't it be awesome if I could start again with all that I now know?* Well, start today.

I'll bet that one or two strategies make a big impression on you right off the bat. Go with them – you are adaptable to circumstance and not a slave to preference. Like coaching, read one per day or week – say on your daily commute – then set your priorities on your daily agenda (I wrote the conversation styles in my notebook and left that page open during meetings). Ask a coach (or anyone) to observe you in action and provide feedback. That'll make the tips and tricks easy to digest and practical to implement. Repeat until they become habitual.

Stick with a strategy anywhere from a month to six, until it becomes automatic and feels normal.

In this series, I'll use myriad examples from the consumer tech, the arts (particularly story-telling) and other industries to illustrate the strategies outlined in each volume. Nevertheless, some will make immediate sense while others will come into play when you move on up.

Self-awareness alone will begin an internal change process that will show on the outside almost immediately – within days.

The series tries to move you quickly into *doing*, because that's vastly more important than simply reading, cogitating, or feeling motivated. I'll give you the *so what?* straight and easy, with real life lessons from some of the toughest work situations.

You'll find a key, which may help you prioritize the strategies:

Easy!	Easy to understand with immediate impact!
Persist	Persist and remain alert. It will deliver!

If this is the first time you've seen this material, it might hurt your head in places as you grapple. Persist and learn more about something that may not resonate at first.

Even if you find something familiar, just re-read it, because reminders are helpful when heads are frantic and memories fade. Consistency and persistence are key.

Now, have a journal handy – it's really important to try the questions if you really want to get the most out of this.

Take your time: remember that *presence* is a panacea. Presence builds resilience when combined with an understanding of your *emotional center* and – as you will read later in Volume 2 – mutually exclusive *options*.

Phew! Now try the exercise below. Look at the following diagram and try to figure out which inner box is a darker shade of grey.

Our Reality is our Perception[1] And Context is King – Which Inner Box is a Lighter Shade of Grey – Left or Right? (answer in the footnote)[2]

Did you get the puzzle?

No two people experience the world in the same way and our priorities, life position and context are all different.

To someone who has everything, everything else looks like opportunity. Conversely, to someone who's simply trying to survive, the exact same things can look like loss prevention. Your context is vital and a strategy may or may not make sense, depending on your life position.

---

[1] New research suggests that what we perceive is in fact a highly veiled reality – the subconscious filters what we're made aware of (without our awareness!) – but that's a whole different science! For now, accept that *our* perception is *our* reality (though perhaps not the *real thing*).

[2] Both inner boxes are the same shade of grey, though the context (outside shades) are different. Nevertheless, you see them differently. Our brains understand anything only by virtue of anything's relationship to anything else and not in absolute terms. Reality looks different to each of us.

Themes

You'll probably notice an underlying theme or two which may surprise you.

Firstly, being impactful requires you to challenge yourself and others – constantly seeking out the best way to do things, rather than just accepting the way things are. This can result in a lot of saying *no* and feeling contrarian.

Consider a statement from the late Steve Jobs, founder and vaunted ex-CEO of Apple and perhaps the most celebrated business leader in modern times: 'What I chose *not* to do was just as important to me as what I *did* do.' Now there's someone with impact!

Paradoxically, his sentiment is of increasing importance for all of us compared to even just half a century back. We now live in a distraction economy which presents us with excessive choice (partly the fault of Steve Jobs, in my view). A lot arrived with the internet, and it's now in our pockets on our smartphones. Every time we're in the company of others and turn to notifications from distant corners of the world, we relinquish easy opportunities to make an impact on those around us. However big or small, these moments add up. Notifications immediately throw us out of presence and when we act like this continuously, we go through a lot of our lives on our own islands with pretend connections. The benefit of saying no will often be freedom to be impactful in our own unique ways where it really counts.

Secondly, you may at first find the strategies make you feel self-centered, or even manipulative in some cases. That's a perfectly normal, but it's not the aim at all. You'll be finding your own voice.

You will also undoubtedly come across some unpalatable truths, particularly when we talk about getting the right things done in Volumes 3 and 4; but also throughout, as we unpack bias and influence. Fear not!

Questions

Before diving in, think now about what impact means to you and what you most want to work on. This will help you to home in on your priorities.

1. What does impact mean to me? ....
2. What do I want to work most on? ....
3. Who could support or help me? ....

Connecting: Self-awareness Behavior & Motivation

Where does this book come from, and what's the role of self-awareness, behavior and motivation in forming impact?

The inspiration for this book came from a role model – sort of a corporate war hero. Let me tell you about resilience under fire – the most enduring leadership lesson in my career.

I was lured in to manage a cost-cutting program for a client whose project was over budget and under-delivering. A Program Director (with arms-length responsibility) and I had to assess the situation quickly and give the client actionable ways of solving his over-spending problem to put the program back on a sound footing.

We gave him the bad news with trepidation.

Shockwaves and recrimination spread through the company we were working for, and as the extent of the broken commitments became clear, trust broke down. Competing suppliers on the program began to muddy the waters, with self-serving interests to take control and to redirect the dwindling program budget in their own direction before the well dried up. Tempers flared when the write-offs began and people retreated into defensive, aggressive and closed behavior. The client lost confidence and feared for his own reputation. The program would have to shed people, some losing their jobs. I was sure I was facing a hell of a year carrying a limping program, and thought the Program Director was in for the axe. I expected him to have a breakdown and recall him throwing his hands up, flustered and resigned, saying 'I don't know' when it all looked like a lost cause.

But he didn't break down…

He turned a break down into breakthrough.

Through most of the serious pressure, he remained poised by our client's side and at his service. He accepted responsibility, re-computed, recalculated, re-formulated, and focused his energy – and intentions – on leading and aligning disparate people, and also not neglecting his *own* needs. He brought together warring suppliers, maintained a positive attitude, presence and understanding of the needs of others. He absorbed and re-directed unsavory behavior to achieve positive outcomes. "Keep your chin up," he would say.

The result was a new program approach, with a different mix of staff and supplier roles. I limped the program back to health. I don't recall if it was saved after I moved on, but I do know that the Program Director's and many other reputations certainly were saved. In fact, he was enhanced, going on to work with the client again. He left an enduring impact, where others would have been slain or fallen by the wayside in a very difficult situation!

Fundamentally, his key success factor was self-awareness and a keen understanding of how stress and negative behavior might have derailed not only himself, but others too, when it all went pear shaped. It allowed him to turn a potential career disaster into a personal triumph. Many of the strategies I learnt during that period are in this book and the remainder of the series. By observing his own behavior, and that of others, he was incredibly present and able to deal with challenges he faced with empathy, skill and clarity. That was the doorway for impact.

Important: keep this story of self-awareness – and how you can avoid tripping yourself up – in mind, as you search for impact value in the strategies.

But what is self-awareness? You could call it impulse control.

Awareness of the limiting behaviors and motivations (mainly your own, but others too) is essential to maximizing impact – otherwise you just get in your own way without knowing it. For instance, when handling difficult circumstances – like change – where strong emotions are in play. You may be threatened by a loss, or motivated by gain. Either way, there will usually be some degree of conflict with others who see things differently. How do you keep a cool head and ensure that not only you, but others too, get what they need?

The most impactful leaders I've seen (not many!) understood the currents below the surface that were informing behavior, and managed it carefully over a sustained period for a positive outcome, when it could have all gone wrong.

In his book *The Obstacle Is The Way* Ryan Holiday talks about difficult situations with a stoic voice. Here's what he says of challenges: '...in these situations, talent is not the most sought after characteristic. Grace and poise are, because these two attributes precede the opportunity to deploy any other skill.'

So, if you don't understand behavior and motivation, you can't get the best out of yourself or anyone else. You'll exit the stage without realizing that you left a perfect opportunity behind. Challenging situations are hard, but they present the *moments* when you show what you're made of.

Here We Are

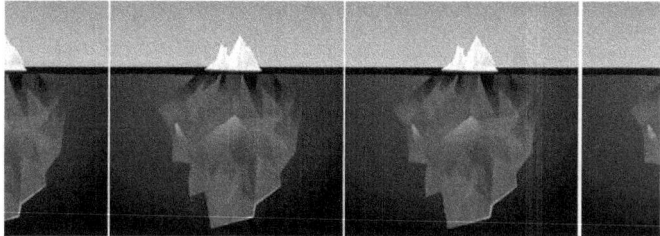

Here we are. You and me. Each of us an iceberg floating in the water.

It may be a surprise to know that virtually all of your behavior originates unseen in your sub-conscious brain, which makes it hard to see the causes and understand them.

What's more, whatever originates in the sub-conscious isn't necessarily logical, analytical or even rational. It results from DNA-level programming and habitual behavior that's been crystallizing inside you since childhood.

Behavior, then, is like an iceberg in the water – virtually all of it lies underneath the waterline.

Unless you know to look down there, you're really just dealing with fragments on the surface – or rationalized facades. Even if you do know to look, you'll find the water's usually murky.

The language of work – visible interactions – is the tip of those icebergs, and it operates in the realm of the rational, analytical, logical and objective. Systems, processes, language and control structures are simply there to facilitate people working together and communicating in a relatively agreeable and predicable fashion. But you'll see, as you read on, that this is mostly veneer. That language masks emotions and habitual behaviors that fundamentally drive humans; and it resides inside the sub-conscious, which is mostly below the surface and disconnected inside its own bubble.[3]

Think of the distinction as wants, which are above the surface in what we articulate to others, and needs, which are below the surface and driven by habits and emotions.

We're not taught ways to frame and articulate complex behavior, beyond perhaps good and bad, helpful or disruptive, or clever or stupid. But these labels are unhelpful because they tell you little about what's actually going on. The only thing you can do with poor information like this is push harder to solve problems; and that's rarely the best answer.

Understanding your automatic behavior, however, stops you from sabotaging yourself, getting into muddle and jumping off a cliff when things go south. If you fail to understand how to get through to others, you may as well be talking to yourself.

---

[3] The tip of the iceberg above the water is relatively new in our evolution – it's called the frontal cortex and is what we see of others. It's what we recognize as *ourselves*, because it constructs and tells the story of us. This is the component that makes us largely distinct from other animals. The part below the waterline is much older - and *is* us. The paradox is that it's the component that's difficult to see easily in ourselves, or even at all in others. We'd probably operate a lot like other animals – largely independent units – if that's all we had. But, it's the part above the water that allows us to construct and tell stories – and that communication enables us to join forces to control resource, in our groups, companies, countries – and run the planet. The singular reason we don't live on *Planet of the Apes* is probably that they can't tell stories like humans can.

You can free yourself to make choices on how to act or react in every situation. You choose exactly how you want to come across to others.

Remember that while success is about *me*, impact is about how you relate to *others*. **You cannot be impactful when understanding or connection are absent.**

So, work through the strategies to understand what really drives your behavior and how to connect with others. The main idea in this volume is to develop your awareness of your own behavior and that of others. It is the key to pretty much everything you will ever do.

Reflection and discussion with a mentor will be enormously helpful to understanding what motivates and drives you. When you understand this, your impact will grow exponentially.

When all is said and done, then, how do you become more self-aware?

The best way to become more self-aware is to take the imaginary camera out of your head and put it up on a balcony.

Turn the spotlight on yourself from a third person's perspective and on others to see the impact you're having. Put the camera on the shoulder of your audience. That situational awareness will provide you with feedback to moderate your own behavior, and this book will show you where it comes from and how you can change it for the better.

Strategy #1: Choose an Optimal Mode of Operation

You'll notice people at work operate in one of four predominant ways in their interaction with others and how they conduct themselves.

Some are analytical and talk in logic, with facts and numbers to hand, while others just want to control everything and make sure everyone's working to plan and procedure. Others still perpetually trumpet new ideas and love an audience for whatever they're thinking. Some love to be connected to others and are happiest when everyone's considered and taken care of.

These four modes of operation aren't exclusive. Each of us will move between them, depending on our role and specific interactions at any time. Even in a *specifically* defined function – say, sales – each of these modes will come into play during different activities and different roles.

You'll notice, however, that one of the four modes dominates how you and others operate most of the time. Understanding these modes is a simple, powerful way to frame preferred, but differing, ways of being.

They guide us towards appropriate behaviors to adopt in different circumstances, and help us connect with others.

Understanding the different modes is especially useful for overcoming blocks in getting through to others; perhaps to your boss. In fact, the more you're able to move around the modes at will, the better.

As you study the diagram below, you'll see yourself and others you know in one or more of these preferred modes. You may also find yourself repelled by one or more that you don't regularly adopt. My advice would be to make them part of your repertoire, because while repulsion and conflict is great on television, it's a million miles from helpful in your career in the real world. Getting along with others really matters off-screen.

Dominant Modes of Operation at Work (And in Life)[4]

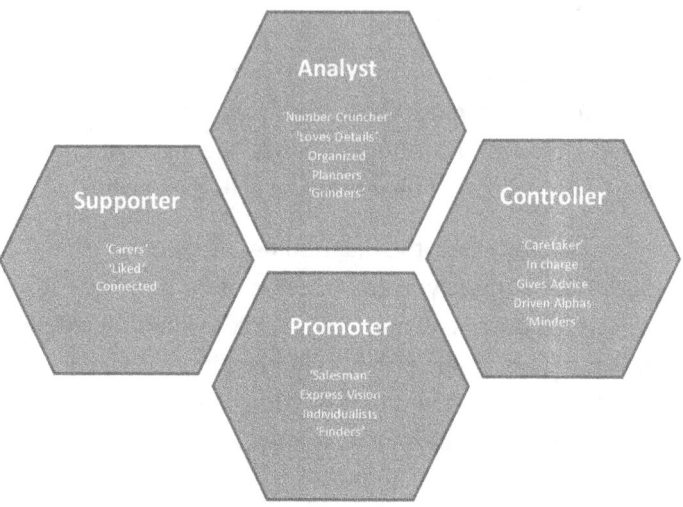

Okay, let's take one of these at a time – and when we do, I want you to try and understand each mode, especially if they aren't you. More importantly, understand how to get through and connect with other modes.

Note: We're going to exaggerate a little and create stereotypes to cover all bases and paint a clear picture of each. The traits in each mode aren't necessarily as blatant as described – except in extreme individuals.

---

[4] You may be familiar with similar models such as NASA's Process Communication Model (PCM)™, and Roger Reid and David Merrill's Social Styles. A more recent Five Factor Model identifies similar traits (author's mapping): Openness & Extraversion (Promoter), Conscientiousness & Introversion (Controller and/or Analyst), Agreeableness (Carer), and Neurotic (perhaps incessant Controller).

Analysts (Number Crunchers)

People in this mode love detail, getting things right and having all their ducks in a row. Analytical types see the world as rules, which, if deciphered or adhered to, lead to achieved goals. They win through logical stories – breaking things down then piecing them back together again. Think of spreadsheets, planners, problem solvers, facts, pros and cons, spider diagrams and so on.

This is the dominant style of corporate worker bees. People in this mode use analysis and objectivity to generate trust in their ideas. This mode is essential for getting objective answers to problems, and these types often end up managing in highly technical industries.

So, what if this is not you? Say it's your team, or boss or a client? You'll need to **appreciate their need for plans, specifics, numbers, structures and clear watertight logic** to stand any chance of getting through in interactions. What you say needs to be coherent, add up and you need to observe the *rules*. You must be analytical in their company, and have a command of the technicalities of the subject at hand.

Try to encourage analysts to make decisions so they don't simply swim and steep in their own analysis for ever. Remember to engage them with puzzles, and motivate them by providing structure to their work.

However, *if this is your dominant mode*, planning, analysis and detail are probably the source of joy unto themselves – but **beware of burying yourself under**

analysis paralysis. Use the 80:20 strategy, explained in Volume 2, to learn when to stop analyzing. The thinking style here tends to focus on detail, expertise and optimization, but you can broaden your capabilities by being more aware of exploring the big picture, creating vision and leading others.

Analysts will probably benefit from Volume 3 on Projecting and Communicating.

Controllers (Caretakers)

These types love to be in charge and typically spend their energy protecting or pushing their agenda. Controllers may be the status quo, in two words.

To Controllers, the world can look like a set of risks and problems to avoid, and they're driven strongly by loss aversion – that is avoiding risk. But they are dedicated, observant, conscientious and committed.

When I think of controllers, I think of caretakers – whose main purpose is to make sure all goes to plan. They're happiest when a well-oiled machine ticks along predictably, according to their mental image. Surprises don't help them, but predictability does. They protect the status quo that they've worked hard to create, so might resist change.

Next to promoters this mode can lack energy and excitement, but it is the dominant style of corporate managers, who are paid to deliver results, reliably. This mode is most useful when things just need to be done and there's no room for negotiation. For instance, if there's a danger to avoid or when time is tight, or even when there's a competitive position to protect.

It's also a style suited to those at the top of their tree who need to defend a hard-won position, whether in a corporate setting or even the de-facto culture of people in a nation.

So, if this is not you, **respect a Controller's need for control and show that you're on top of whatever it is that you're doing** to get through to them. Be concise, confident, and direct in your communication. Shrinking violets beware: you will fail to get through to Controllers unless you match their mode. They are most engaged by dependable people who operate like a Swiss clock.

You can light a fire underneath them, simply by demonstrating a potential for loss from inaction.

If this is your dominant mode, **remember to get and to give support. Get out of your own head and engage people as people**, with their myriad wants, needs and perspectives; and without judgment. Engage differing opinions and avoid stress by letting go of things you don't control. The thinking style here tends to focus on detail, process, planning, taking action and optimization, but you can broaden your capabilities through connecting with – and coaching – others.

As a manager, remember to trust people if you want them to be trustworthy – people automatically behave according to the identity you create with them.

Also recognize how challenged you will feel by Promoters (who naturally challenge the status quo).

If Controller is the de-facto culture and market position of your organization, realize that you will be challenged by upstart Promoter organizations (known as the Innovator's Dilemma).

You may have surmised, thus far, that Analytical and Controlling is a common combination of modes in the corporate workplace. My teams would have concurred that my own behavior shifted between these two most strongly during my career (and my family might volunteer that that's still the case)! Look now at your own behavior – are you one or both?

Though I found these styles highly effective most of the time, it wasn't until I needed to break through into the ranks of senior leadership that they alone became limiting. What I needed was more promoting and supporting, which I went on to practice more consciously and consistently.

Controllers will love Volume 4 on competing (though your boss might not appreciate it quite as much)!

Promoters (Salesmen or Creatives)

Where Controllers often love a status quo, Promoters love change and new ideas. In a word, they are disrupters and see the world as a multitude of opportunities.

Think of salesmen, politicians, visionaries, creatives, entrepreneurs and other smooth talkers. Put simply, these types are happiest being spontaneous, espousing their latest, greatest idea. They're typically found in politics and senior corporate leadership and are the mainstay of entrepreneurship, celebrity, entertainment and media too.

These types often feel like they have to drag the rest of us into the new century, however, they sometimes get so wrapped up in their own *ideas* they're don't knuckle down and *deliver*. They get their dopamine hit from the idea and not necessarily the execution.

This mode is most useful when selling new ideas, at a point in time when delivery doesn't yet matter.

If this is not you, **remember to pitch up with energy, passion and excitement** to get through to them. When you *just don't get it*, they'll leave you for dead.

Promoters tend to take the risks in life, but dragging the rest of us along is never easy. There may be battle scars and painful wounds underneath a confident sales façade. But you'll motivate them through talk of opportunity.

Controllers (caretakers) often feel challenged by Promoters, and the pair of them will pull in different directions – epitomized by status quo versus disruptive upstart. Analysts – searching for detail, logical constraints and broken rules – tend to bore the pants off Promoters.

Beware, however, Promoters may not show up to an engagement as promised, and you may find their attention fleeting. They may not be particularly dependable as they flit from idea to idea. Ensure they get specific and realistic, while you also recognize their creative energy. If you're being promoted to, ensure there's sufficient resource and process to complete what's committed.

At the very least, try to pretend they are unique.

If this is your dominant style, **beware the need to deliver on commitments and to work on dependability.** Volume 2 is for you and will give you a ready process. You could team up with someone who will do the work – entertainers, creatives and startups do this frequently. The thinking style here tends to focus on exploring the big picture, visioning and connecting to others, but you can broaden your capabilities through more detailed process, action and expertise.

Be sure to invite reality checks of your ideas however painful that might feel. Learn to get comfortable with objectivity, detail and good process in your work and delegate these roles and tasks to others if you must. Good ideas are underpinned by solid analysis, numbers and logic.

Accept also that everyone sits on a bell curve, and that caretakers in particular simply won't move left or right of center quick enough for you – if ever. Humans are risk-averse and ideas often succeed through evolution, not revolution, even if that takes a long, long time. Change, for the vast majority, is simply the stuff of dreamland and little more than a topic of conversation.

Finally, give Analysts something tangible to get excited about or they will just see fluff.

As I personally opened up to and experienced Promoting roles at work, I began to find my true mode for the right stage in my career. It felt engaging and comfortable. It opened my eyes to the possibility that the Analytical mode, in particular, was learnt behavior for me, adopted for my circumstances at the time. Producing these coaching guides supports my aim to become more promoting too.

As you move around the modes, you may discover a skill or passion you've never truly made the most of. So, try roles in different modes and see what happens.

As we've said, Volume 2 on achieving notable goals will benefit Promoters.

Supporters (Carers or Connectors)

More than anything, these types love to help and support others to get what they need. Supporters are warm and friendly and see the world as a network of feelings. They win through connections, they're charitable and their primary need is to know that everyone's happy, or at least okay. They feel best when they have a close community. This mode is most useful for coaching others.

Out and out Supporters are rarely visible in corporate culture, in which *me, me, me* is the prevailing mode. It's rarely, if ever, seen in senior corporate management, because those jobs have traditionally entailed controlling and cutting, rather than supporting.

If this is not you, perhaps all you need to do is to pitch up with a problem the supporter can help with; beware though, you may be expected to drench them with gratitude when they do help. You can also help yourself enormously by acting with warmth towards others if you want real engagement – there's nothing quite as inviting. Equally, there's little as flat as continuously stern. I've seen this trait used to great effect by a top city lawyer who lectured me at university. Though undoubtedly very bright and successful, given her position, it was her warmth towards the students and her colleagues that everyone remembered first. Controllers and analysts can learn a great deal from her endearing style.

Remember that these types can be the social glue in fractious circumstances. They may be the only ones who listen enough to what's really going on, so they're often key in calming tensions when everyone else's trying to promote, control, or analyze their way out of a sticky situation. Connect with these types on a personal level, but watch out for their self-deprecation.

If this is your dominant style, **remember the need to look after your own needs as well as those of** others. **Try not to get dumped on, and try not to forget that most people are simply not as thoughtful as you may be.** The thinking style here tends to focus on relationships and supporting others, but you can broaden your capabilities through more detailed process and action as well as exploring the bigger picture.

While a Supporter-only mode is rarely seen in corporate leadership, the irony I think is that this (along with Promoting), is the style to unlock leadership and create the distinction between management. When you read about leadership in Volume 3, you'll see that the best leaders know that they need to spend time as Supporters, even if it's not their preferred mode of operation.

Supporters may benefit from looking at Volume 4 on Competing – though they may not appreciate the sentiments. But they will benefit from understanding that impact requires them to look after their own interests too.

So, with all that said, what can you do with operating modes?

First, identify your dominant modes and see if you're covering the right bases for your role. Remember, the modes you normally use may be heavily influenced by your work and may not be your naturally preferred modes. If you're frustrated or unhappy at work, this may be a key – you might simply be wearing the wrong trousers. Which of these modes would you stop being if given half a chance? Whatever's left may be the sort of role you should seek.

Second, observe your own behavior and shore up where you're lacking. Impact frequently requires you to face up to challenges outside your little box and you may find that you can operate perfectly well outside it, with spectacular impact (for a time, at least). To become more y*ou,* you may need to adopt a mode you're not currently using. For instance, I made more time for coaching and socializing with my teams to adopt a more Supporting mode. To become more Promoting, I chose to developing new business and pitch innovative solutions to corporate problems.

Third, observe those who are most important to you, and understand which mode they use when interacting. The more self-aware they are, the more likely it is that their mode will vary according to the situation. Impactful people adjust their behavior and learn to acknowledge, but set aside their preferences when they don't suit their purpose. Mimic their preferred modes whenever you really need to get through to them.

Finally, try building more effective teams around operating modes. For instance, if you have a highly controlling or analytical client, your team's going to have a hard time if it's led only by Promoters. A common mistake is where salesmen (read Promoter) move on to manage deliveries (read Controller) of new engagements, but fail to transition from their default mode to the appropriate mode for the activity.

Questions

Now think about and identify your predominant modes and those around you.

1. My dominant modes of operation: ....

2. My preferred modes of operation or what would I like more of: ....

3. How I will address the gap: ....

4. The dominant modes of key people around me at work: ...

5. How I will match their mode in interaction: ....

6. How I will diversify my team to incorporate the different modes appropriately: ....

Strategy #2: Your Inner Parent, Adult and Child

From day one, we all have to learn how to get what we want from those around us.

A lot of what we learn, as children, then becomes habitual and ingrained in our subconscious thinking.

In fact, our ways of thinking are a lot like any other habits when performed repeatedly over a long period. Our brains literally wire themselves to think and interact with the world in the ways we hone, day after day, over a lifetime.

As we grow through various roles in our lives, we pick up new habitual patterns of thinking to get what we want along the way.

Eventually, everyone comes to work with a different mix of what's called Parent, Adult and Child inside.

These are known as ego states and were framed by Eric Berne in the 1950s.

Good or bad, you'll see myriad habitual thinking habits play out in behaviors at work every day. Most of it happens without conscious awareness, so it's hard to see precisely what's going on.

Parent Adult Child – The myriad ways of interacting to get what we want[5]

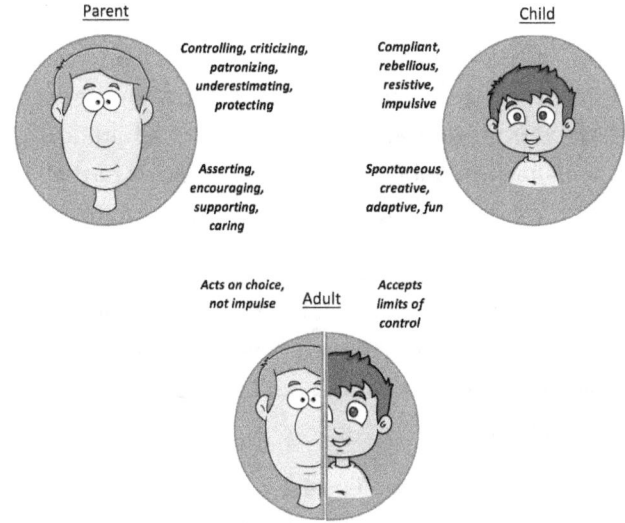

Let's start at the beginning – and grow as we go!

---

[5] Parent Adult Child is part of Transactional Analysis, framed by Eric Berne in the 1950s

Child

To get what we want, we start out being:

- **Compliant** and **rebellious** at times
- More positively **spontaneous (free spirited)** and **adaptable**

If you look around your office, you'll probably observe these behaviors still playing out to greater or lesser extent in interactions every day. By adulthood, these behaviors, adopted from the beginning of time, are firmly wired into our brains and become automatic.

The potentially destructive elements (unbridled compliance or rebelliousness) are most noticeable in grown-ups when you see them, metaphorically speaking, *throwing their toys out of the pram* having not gotten their way.

Excessive Compliance usually reveals itself in adults who don't speak up, even when they have a relevant point of view. The latter then comes with an excessive need to do whatever they're told in order to be accepted or valued.

It's not hard to see how these automatic behaviors take seed in the parenting we receive as children. It's also not hard to see how they can seriously work against us as adults. Awareness is vital for us to make good choices.

What's more, when we act as Child towards others, their natural instinct is to act Parent back towards us – it's a natural co-existence which is comfortable, familiar and automatic to all of us.

Nevertheless, we have to be careful not to inadvertently trigger Parenting treatment, which we don't necessarily want from others.

Parent

As children, we may experience:

- Excessively **controlling, protective** or **patronizing** parenting
- More positive **assertive, encouraging** and **caring** parents

As children, we simply learn to emulate what we see in the guardians of our little lives, then act out the part we've learnt with our own children and other little elves that we look after as adults (such as your team at work). Again, look around the office and you'll see these behaviors play out all around you.

The potentially destructive elements in Parent (excessive control, protection or patronizing) are most noticeable when adults don't control what they feel they are *entitled* to. Adults often become obsessively controlling over what they can't realistically control, belittling others who don't meet expectations – or they become overly protective of someone perceived as vulnerable. An obvious example is an office manager who can't free the reigns and delegate to his or her team.

As with Child, when we act as Parent to others their natural instinct is to act as Child back to us. Excessive Controllers might revel in the feeling of little elves running around their feet, but may also find themselves shouldering burdens alone, when others are too afraid to speak up or take responsibility for what they do.

Adult

And lastly, adult.

Most of us grow up to learn that we can choose our behavior and don't *have to* follow primeval instincts alone.

As **rational Adults**, we recognize and accept that everyone – like us – is entitled to their own free choice.

When you operate from this realm, you accept the limits of your control depending upon the situation.

As an adult, you are more likely to consider and listen to other options and negotiate for what you want, so that both sides in a transaction get what they need. Sometimes you *accept* that it may not be possible to get what you want.

So, to now make Parent Adult Child more real, here are some further scenarios from the office:

- Imagine you act as *helpless Child* to get assistance from your colleagues. They have a natural tendency to act as Parent. Through reciprocity, they help you repeatedly.
- You can lighten a relationship and create connection by deliberately acting as *fun-loving Child,* or luring it out of others at times. This creates intimacy and play, which is great for those who've long forgotten what that feels like!
- You might act as a *highly controlling Parent* to get what you want, if and when there isn't time for a discussion.

So, how do you manage your Parent, Adult and Child inside?

1) Just like operating modes in strategy #1, **understanding where you normally operate from can help to identify behavior that works for and against you.** Is there a particular person, with a particular mode that brings out the worst in you against your better judgment?

   By way of example, I once had an intimidatingly large job to run a horrifically difficult program, to transform part of a global company. The program leader's default style, with me at least, was one of *highly Controlling Parent* (I've combined Operating Modes with Parent Adult Child in this example). This is a fairly normal style for corporate senior managers, and is exacerbated during the stressful, demanding situations which they usually find themselves in.

This leader, however, was off the control scale! He would patronize and belittle constantly – and not just with me. He provided little support or understanding and was incredibly demanding and unforgiving. On some Monday mornings it felt like agony just getting on the plane to work. By Wednesday I was usually just relieved to have checked-in online for the flight home, albeit departing on Thursday!

So how did I *react* to this? I'm no shrinking violet and didn't have the disease to please, so I would repeatedly push back against unreasonable demands in the most civil way I could. I'd offer suggestions for doing things a better way, hoping to move the relationship to *Adult-Adult*. That sounds reasonable, does it not? He, however, would often overrule me in meetings with our team, and it felt to me that we clashed constantly. What this did to me was bring out the *Rebellious Child* – that's my default reaction to highly controlling managers. It may not have been the best response.

2) **It's usually best to break out of a Parent-Child interaction when it starts to becomes the norm.** Such behavior cements surprisingly quickly and sets extremely hard. Because of its primeval nature, it

can be difficult to break the habit when one of the duo hasn't matured, but the other has.

Continuing the example from the previous bullet, my boss was obviously in charge and I eventually relented, knuckling down and working 18-20 hour days to meet as many of his demands as I physically could. My reaction smoothed the ruffles – he felt better and I felt slightly less harassed! And we even began to share jokes at one point. It felt like we'd reached a turning point and an understanding of how to work together.

Except that it wasn't quite what it seemed. Before long, my *compliance* led to further demands. My behavior had become *Compliant Child*, a relationship pattern which worked well for him, but made it harder for me to resist unreasonable demands.

Again, I realized that that wasn't a sustainable behavior, so I pulled the plug and eventually exited the project – a choice partly from my *Adult* and partly from my *Rebellious Child*. It seemed to me that he couldn't break out of *Controlling Parent*.

I have since had a team member who found herself working with a different highly controlling manager (they're everywhere, unfortunately!) and the same cycle looked to be developing once again, in the same way. Except this time, with the benefit of awareness (my team member's incessant tiredness, and midnight emailing) and appropriate intervention from her line manager, the differences were short-lived by both sides. The key to success here was manifold. First, my team member was aware that it was partly her own action (excessive compliance) which allowed and reinforced the unwelcome reaction (excessive control). Second, the demands on her time required at least some analytical validation, perhaps with the support of her manager, before blind acceptance. Third, her work ethic was a strength when purposed in a productive way. In this instance, she also took on assertiveness training to learn to avoid setting, or walking into unrealistic expectations – and to break unhealthy relationships by moving them to an Adult-Adult footing. Needless to say, it took time and persistence to develop these skills. You can read about assertiveness in Volume 3.

The first situation described here – my troubles with a difficult project based boss – involved a smart man who knew what he was doing and he was clearly a highly *Controlling* alpha leader – these types may well push your buttons in the same way to get what they want. The second situation involved a manager who was clueless to the effect they were having on their team member – though I wasn't. I managed to rescue a difficult situation by understanding reactions and seeing where my team member needed to take action and seek support.

Beware and be prepared. Look around the office and see what your colleagues and bosses are doing. Your aim is to move your office interactions towards Adult-Adult.

Do a post mortem of your work and projects over the last few years. What worked? What brought out the best or worst in you, and why? Does a *Controlling Parent* style (the de facto style of corporate managers) bring out the *Rebellious Child* in you, like it did in me?

3) It's rarely possible to change another's interaction style simply by knowing about Parent Adult Child, **so the best remedy is often to gather good feedback on what works and what doesn't, as well as outside coaching support**. If a change in the relationship is unavoidable, provide clear, honest intentions for change early on, try to make it happen, but ultimately, move on if you see no change. Just accept that working with some people is going to be more trouble than it is worth.

Questions

Like before, think about and identify your predominant modes and those of the people around you.

1. The interaction I'm most concerned about is/are: ....
2. My normal mode in these interactions is (Parent/Adult/Child): ....
3. My 'opponent's' mode is (Parent/Adult/Child): ....
4. My automatic behavior: ....
5. Similar circumstances in my career: ....
6. Observable patterns: ....
7. Combination with operating mode (e.g. Controlling Parent): ....
8. My actions to address the concerns (feedback, mentoring, support, change of mode (Adult-Adult), walk-away, etc): ....

Strategy #3: I'm Okay? Are You Okay?

We all take one of four life positions, whether or not we are aware of it. Formed through our interactions, the parenting we receive and habitual ways of thinking, our brains literally wire themselves to play out what we've *learnt* to believe. We end up with a self-image or worldview.

As an adult, our life position determines how we come across to others in every interaction.

These positions are called I'm Okay, You're Okay, and they all happen without our awareness.

Life Positions – How We Feel About Ourselves In Relation To Others

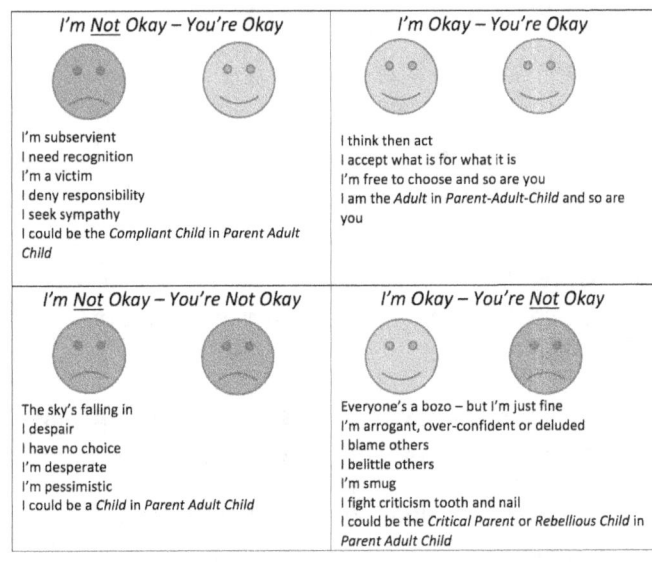

Can you see yourself in one of these positions? Ask family and friends what they see in you – perhaps anonymously, if you really want an objective opinion. There's a good chance they'll have a better idea of you than you do – or at least a good perspective.

Changing a life position isn't quick or easy, because the behavioral patterns in your brain are already set.

Simply be aware of your default behavior and learn to recognize assumptions and separate them from fact.

That awareness will itself begin a change and open up the choice to act differently when things aren't working.

You'll need to isolate the stories you create in your head, versus what's definitively, observably real, right in front of you.

When you look at the attributes in the table above, it's easy to see that most of these life positions are based on assumption – not fact. **Learn to exercise choice over your behavior** and it will become automatic over time.

Beware a couple of things. It's tempting and common to overcompensate when trying to move out of an I'm Not Okay position, consciously and analytically. That is to say, it's easy to try and claw back respect that has been lost over time and move into an I'm Okay, You're Not Okay position. This is a defensive stance against possible past injustice. Simply be aware so that it doesn't backfire on you. **Remember to aim always for I'm Okay, You're Okay when you look at the world and other people.**

Also be aware that when you change, others will resist. That's because the way in which they see you and interact with you will also have cemented inside their heads. Change is uncomfortable and not always welcome, but they'll have to change with you in order to work better with you.

Coming back to the highly controlling leader that I introduced in operating modes, it's probable that

that mode came with a worldview of 'I'm Okay, You're not Okay.' It's probable also that that was combined with a controlling Parent mode of interaction from the previous strategy. Can you see how these may combine to form a persona?

Questions

1. My normal life position is: ....
2. The impact this has on my interactions: ....
3. Combination with my operating mode (e.g. *Controlling* + I'm Okay, You're Not Okay): ....
4. Combination with Parent Adult Child (e.g. *Controlling* or *Patronizing Parent* and I'm Okay, You're Not Okay): ....
5. Similar circumstances in my career: ....
6. Observable patterns: ....
7. Actions to move to I'm Okay, You're Okay: ....
8. My actions to address the concerns (feedback, mentoring, support, change of mode, walk- away, etc: . ...

Strategy #4: The Right Relationships are Everything

Unless you have sufficient resource to do your own thing – alone probably – you'll need others to survive and also to thrive. Obviously, money's required to pay bills, customers must exist to buy your products and peers need to buy-in to your ideas. You'll also need others to enjoy life with and products to have fun with. It's a virtuous circle.

    Now, think back to when you first joined an office. Like most people early in their careers, you probably began to feel that it wasn't what you knew, but who you knew. Though that may sound repulsive, there's a truth as fundamental as DNA in there, and despite the myriad Human Resource and Performance Management processes we'll ever reinvent for ourselves, that's one truth that's guaranteed to never change.

What It Takes to Be Human: The Worker Bee Model

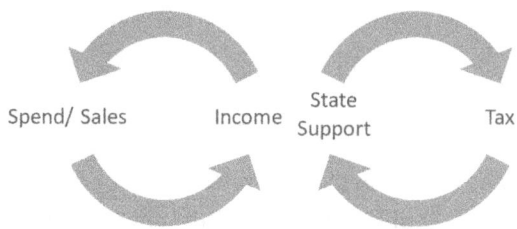

The relationship seems so obvious, that it's easy to take for granted.

Is there anything that we do that isn't underpinned by this complete cycle?

It underlies everything, but the point here is that **you need good relationships *more than you need anything else,*** or this fundamental cycle stops working for you. None of the individual bits work without relationships and the mutual dependence is unshakeable. So the better your relationships, within this cycle, the easier it will be to impact more people.

Remember we said impact is about how well **you can get others to move for your wants and desires in the introduction? People (relationships) are your most fundamental resource. To listeners, you tell stories, and stories are the only things that turn the world on its axis – so far as anyone will ever know or care!**

Just as important though, the best business relationships provide you with something called *social proof*, which is the most powerful way of building a truly impactful reputation. Put simply, social proof is someone else vouching for you.

Some people describe themselves as relational beings, feeling valued and happy when interactions are going well, but feeling down when they aren't. Others seem to get more value and energy from doing, creating or achieving, perhaps on their own or with inanimate objects, but paying scant attention to others around them.

If you are a *relational* being, don't forget that you need to create real stuff of value which other people actually want at work.

If you are a *doer*, it pays to remember to acknowledge others too at work, and to take them along your journey with you – after all, nothing is possible without at least a handful of them.

So, how do we find and make the right relationships? Should they all be deep? Or shallow? It's hard to put a finger on what's right, especially for those who aren't relational beings. Just knowing what we want from our relationships can be surprisingly hard, but putting in too little or too much can yield unwelcome results.

There's a popular saying that *you're the product of the five people around you,* and that sounds like what's known as an inner circle. If you want to have impact at work, your aim is to get inside inner circles of control, because they typically shape agendas. When you're not inside an inner circle, you're being controlled. But all that is still an imprecise way of figuring out what you want from relationships.

So, relationships can be grouped into four main types. Understanding these can help you figure out what you want and what's appropriate for your interactions – that is to say, what you should expect to put in and get out.

Four Relationship Types

Transactional	Dependent
"Cold"	*"Hot"*
Necessary to get your work done	You frequently work/socialise with them
Pay your bills, etc	May spend a lot of time together
No reason to have a beer with them	Genuinely depend on each other
Chance encounters or necessary evils	Mutual respect, tolerance of differences and connection are important
Casual	Social
"Cool"	*"Warm"*
Occasional encounters - stop to say hello	Best friends – you want to have fun with them
No particular need of them	Shoulder to lean on
Peripheral to each other	May be open - sometimes more than with Dependents
Receptionists, people at conferences and training events	

Think about your relationships and see if your wishes match the description. Consider the following:

- Do you spend excessive time on Transactional and Casual relationships (perhaps at work or on social media) and not enough on Dependents (perhaps at home)?
- A relationship with your boss is Dependent – do both sides treat it as such, or is it always one way? Is it just giving or just taking? Are you being too social with a boss and not sufficiently strategic?
- Is someone behaving unexpectedly coldly towards you? Could they see your relationship as Transactional or Casual, whereas you see it as Social or Dependent?
- Equally, is someone over-familiar and awkward all the time? Are they trying to get closer and are you doing something that might mislead them?
- Where do you need to invest more or less of your time and energy?

So, how do you invest more or less and move your relationships to where you want them? A concept known as Psychic Distance from creative writing can help us understand how to do this, when combined with the relationship model above.

Psychic Distance and Expectations

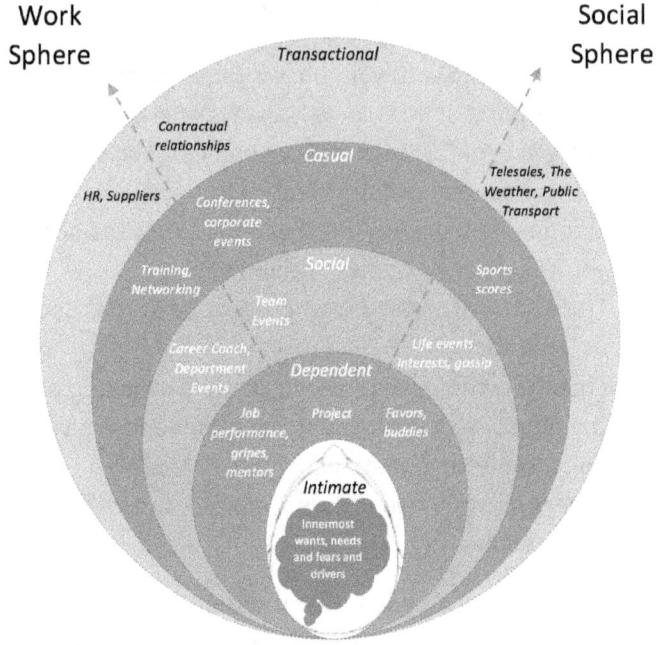

You can see from the diagram above, that it's perfectly possible to understand professional and social relationships in a tangible way, rather than having to muddle through and hope for the best.

A few things stand out:

- **We all expect to be more closed to those who are distant from us**
- Professional relationships tend to permeate the outer transactional edges of psychic distance, whereas frequent interactions tend to be more social and come with the expectation of openness and intimacy
- In terms of relationship style, what's appropriate for professional distance is inappropriate for family interaction
- Conversely, being an open book at work may be just as inappropriate. Nevertheless, remaining distant from those you most frequently work with may feel odd to them too. You have to find the right balance of intimacy and distance, depending on the culture.

Cultural influences on the interaction model are significant and interaction norms can vary significantly. Have you ever noticed how some people, being well-meaning and friendly, start conversations on public transport? In these scenarios, they're getting Social, whereas you're expecting Transactional, or even less, especially if you're on autopilot inside your own head.

In another example, presenters sometimes begin their pitch with intimate, personal stories to try and make a connection with their audiences straight away. That does sound phony to some, like a sales pitch, but can be heartwarming to others.

The key point is that it's generally uncomfortable to go straight from the outside circle, to the inner circle and vice versa. When this leap back and forth is frequent, it's usually interpreted by the recipient as someone blowing hot and cold.

At the same time, if you want to get close to others and extract a personal revelation, or even if you want to make them *feel* special, then you need to bring them into your center.

This is usually how leaders engage others. In a sense, you're revealing your authentic self, which is normally a closed door and it can feel like a privilege to be let in. Beware though, if you later close the door, they will almost certainly feel manipulated.

Some advice:

- Move relationships toward the center or outer edge one step at a time. If you want to end a relationship, move the other person towards the outer edge *slowly*. Over time, intimacy diminishes naturally like old friends parting ways after school. As soon as you make it Transactional, their sub-conscious will get the message
- Remember to mirror the appropriate level of intimacy in your relationships
- Interact at least socially for relationships to feel intimate
- Express increasing empathy as you move towards someone's center. You're heading into their humanity, with all its frailty and vulnerability

- The center is where reality begins and ends. Conversely, the further away you are from the center, the more you're looking at stories, dressing, masks and facades (more about story-telling in Volume 3)
- Don't be offended if you're treated coldly by someone when you first meet them – a first exchange is usually Transactional. Just understand that your relationship expectations may be unrealistic, and move it systematically over time to where you want it
- Beware of becoming limited by forming ideas. When you read the Ladder of Interference below, you'll understand that we get stuck on our ideas and interpretations and find it difficult to break free. The implication is that your friends, family and co-workers will have formed fixed ideas about you, and that can be limiting when you want to grow and develop beyond what they want to see. An easily understood example of this is with highly branded public figures – they invariably have a hard time diversifying into other realms of life, because we get fixated on what they represent to us. Development and growth requires you to have new people around you, and sometimes, to move on from those with old ideas. Moving within or outside your organization can be an effective way to offload relationship shackles – but you may be starting again in some senses. If you do move, don't give up on relationships you've spent years building. Evolving to a supplier/buyer from a boss/employee relationship can be a rewarding shift.

- Don't confuse *social networks* for *social or intimate relationships*. You can see that they are – for the most part – transactional and casual in terms of psychic distance. That means you're almost certain to face façades, dressing up and marketing, so don't misjudge and post whatever's most intimate.
- Remember, warmth is endearing. Perpetually controlling and analytical are cold and transactional. We'll talk about this more when we look at trust in Volume 3.

Questions

1. My key relationships which require work: ....
2. Current and expected psychic distance: ....
3. What I will do to alter these relationships? ....

Strategy #5: What Motivates You? What Do You Really Value?

One of the commonest challenges for most people is simply enjoying the work they do. A vast majority of us seem to spend our entire time wishing for something else. We're envious of people who find their sweet spot, because we hear enthusiasm for what they do in the stories they tell.

However, many of us have heard of people who've worked forty years in a job, of which they hated every minute. That's the antithesis of impact and sounds like a lifetime squandered.

Impact, however, is taking full responsibility for what you do – without internal reservation – and that's essential for impact. It's the only way to avoid an invisible ceiling when you're climbing the ladder.

This will be reinforced by the triage, which we will cover in Volume 2.

How do you avoid simply becoming a wage slave to something you dislike, or even hate? *Part* of the answer is learning to say no to what you don't want; but more on that later. Here, we'll now look at motivation – how to find it, then chase it down.

Key Sources of Motivation at Work[6]

During your early years at work, it's enormously helpful to get brand affiliation on your resume. It'll help you get established and to be part of something that you can tell and sell on. In the latter years, motivators shift

---

[6] A) The mainstay of corporate life. Some places trowel out non-serial achievers! Strongly reinforced by schooling and community. B) Source of indirect power when you trade something or some input with your connections. C) The ultimate motivator. Nothing finds a pulse faster, though it's neither pleasant nor sustainable. D) Perhaps the ultimate aim. Easily deferred and made contingent on future achievements. Can also be a middle-class trap. E) Unusually the preserve of entrepreneurs. Often the strongest proponents of 'purpose.' F) The easiest way to build a reputation. However, evidence of your worthiness is in someone else's hands. Evolves with self-confidence and age. G) Like F, someone else is in control. Evolves with self-confidence and age.

towards seeing out retirement and locking in a good pension. Middle agers want to earn a lot while they still can and also want to cement a legacy before they run out of time.

Recognize the distinction between positive and negative motivation. The former is about chasing some good – say position or status. The latter is driven by fear – loss of income or status. Think carrot versus stick. While positive motivators are more sustainable, negative motivators are much more powerful in the moment. We are loss-averse creatures, but that aversion can only work in short sharp busts. You can use negative motivation to get yourself or others to change, do something, or to get things started quickly, but default back to positive motivators to keep things moving.

Now – purpose.

The need for some kind of *purpose* in our work feels like a relatively new phenomenon. It's the idea that work should have some broader, irreverent value, beyond simply bringing home the bacon. But this hasn't always been a significant need – those of yesteryear (and many people still today) were often simply happy to have paid dependable work.

But with work now dominating our lives so completely, and almost semi-religiously for many, other sources of **life purpose seem to have been vanquished**. In addition, certainly in wealthier countries, secure roofs over heads, food on tables, good health and education have freed our minds to wander to more fanciful ideas like *purpose*. And while we've begun to believe headlines when they tell us that we can – individually – change the world, the comforting certainty of a fixed life position has gone with it, leaving a void of uncertainty. All of that change means we face the lure of abundance and seemingly free choice, but without solid ground to stand on. How do we navigate open choice without regret for making the wrong one? Well, we invent *purpose* to re-constrain our path and provide a feeling of certainty once again.

Purpose, then, seems to provide direction amongst seemingly endless options and also comes with the chance to avoid regret. It appears to be the result of our evolving beyond basic needs, but serves our innate desire for clarity. Whatever the reason, **surveys consistently show that *purpose* is a vital motivator along with recognition.**

Purposeful people from history were usually self-directed. Think of scientists, engineers, world leaders, philanthropists, entertainers and so on, who made a notable impact on the world. Entrepreneurs also fall in this category and a common component of these roles is freedom and autonomy. But this idea applies to corporate professionals as well. Think of it as taking personal responsibility for what you choose to do, how you choose to do it, and with whom. It doesn't mean being self-centered or going it alone, but instead taking control of what you represent to bring out the best in you.

What motivates you to get out of bed most days – even on the cold, dark, rainy winter mornings? Has that changed as your needs were ticked-off, or as you grew throughout your career?

Look at the circles and figure out what fundamentally drives you. Which of these circles gives you a repeated dopamine hit or brings much needed comfort?

Hollywood composer Hans Zimmer talks about the process of *hunting* down a *specific* sound for his for his incredible compositions. Though that sounds incredibly painstaking (the process – not the music), his dopamine system is probably out hunting for a dopamine hit. That's like panning for gold. Writers – and their readers – may chase the perfect scene, line or phrase, creating or combing through tomes repeatedly to find their hit.

Which of the motivators above were at play when you did your best work, or your worst work? Do you get that in your current work? Journal your thoughts, and expect to take weeks – or possibly months – to figure what motivates you. Getting fundamental takes time. Ask yourself, in the key circumstances of your work, which of these were you aiming for? What was the underlying retreated pattern?

Persist, to understand your underlying motivators. For example, being financially motivated is commonly the result of social pressure, so the motivation is really to fit in or look successful and not the financial success itself. One of my coachees found –

after six months of questioning and identifying when she was happiest – that she desired autonomy more than money. She made a tradeoff and left the company to start her own business. The rule is to keep questioning your motivators. If your environment doesn't support your motivators, it may be time to move out and go somewhere that does.

But while surface wants can be easily articulated, subconscious needs – which really are the drivers of motivation – can be hard to unearth. Try these questions:

1) What can you talk about all day, everyday, and bore the pants off someone with?
2) What did you spend your time doing when you were pre-teen? We normally get lost in responsibilities of the world after that age
3) Imagine your tombstone. If there's just one accolade you could have, what would it say? That you were persistent at balancing accounts? Sounds unlikely. So, what *should* it say?

When you think about and answer these questions honestly, your subconscious will act on them imperceptibly. You'll find your mind conjuring up actions to point you in the right direction almost immediately. Most of all, you'll feel a clarity and focus like you may never have had before, especially if you've been in a role that doesn't suit you. As a side benefit it will become much easier to then say no to what you don't value. More on that later.

Some final observations:

- If the only thing you need is an income, avoid a job which demands passion and a sense of purpose, because it will be difficult to keep up the pretense for something that isn't passion worthy
- If you value simplicity and predictability, find a role that's all about repeatable process and let the process do the work. Luckily, 95% of jobs are of this nature, because routine keeps the bills paid. The downside is that big impact is rarely found in an easily repeatable process
- If you value freedom and autonomy, you're going to have a hard time with Controllers, caretakers and micro-managers. You can double that if you're a natural Promoter. What this book helps you to do is make a choice between walking away and using the strategies to help to make the most of whatever you decide to stick with
- Invent a purpose to point you in a direction, but remember that salaried corporate jobs really only exist because they turn a profit for shareholders. When profitability disappears, any notion of purpose tends to go with it and the waters close behind surprisingly quickly
- Understanding your own motivators can help you come back to your own emotional center at the end of the day and temporarily disregard the rest of the world and what it's up to. This can help to negate comparison based judgments, which often lead to dissatisfaction and serve the interests of others

marketing their own ideas. It's easier to find your emotional center when you do what motivates you and make meaningful progress doing it.

Questions

1. My key motivators from the diagram: ....

2. Underlying motivators behind them, after more thought:

   ....

3. How I will attract more of these in my work?

   ....

Strategy #6: What Drives You?

Okay, so now we're going to consider another perspective on what drives our behavior.

Perhaps the defining characteristic of humanity is the need for *validation*.

It seems that whatever we do, it's all about being valued by ourselves and others. We spend a lifetime racing to collect resource for that purpose alone (wealth, property, relationships, careers and so on). Along the way we amass experiences and form assumptions about the world, which then shape our beliefs. We then use those beliefs to attract more of the resource that makes us feel valued. It all starts early in life, when we see the behavior of our own parents and community – and the results that their behavior yields.

For instance, if our being top of the class is the only thing that brings praise from our parents and community, we may learn that being valued means 'being perfect' in all that we do. If our parents praise us for our independence, we may learn that we need to 'be strong' in all that we do. Those beliefs continue to play out in adulthood and are exacerbated by the cultural norms of the organizations we work for.

When talking about cultural *fit* for a role, these drivers can be a surprisingly – and perhaps worryingly – good place to look.

TA[7] Drivers – How We Feel Valued

Please Me/Others
I'm caring and considerate
I have the 'Disease to Please'
I'm happy when everyone is
I avoid conflict
I dislike being ignored

Be Perfect
I'm a high achiever
I have to be right and must win
I berate myself for falling short
I dislike emotional people and slackers
I want control
I need accolades and trophies

Be Strong
I'm brave
I'm independent and self-sufficient
I'm emotionless and closed
I won't ask for help
I like saving the day
I like dependents (cowering preferably)!

Try Hard
I'm ambitious and determined
I persist in the face of difficulties
I wear workaholic as a badge of honour
I dislike my effort going unnoticed
It's good to be first in and last out

Hurry Up
Let's be quick - there isn't time
I'm efficient and responsive
I get impatient with details and slow coaches
I dislike thumb twiddling
I like outpacing others and being first

---

[7] Transactional Analysis - Eric Berne

One or more of these drivers probably dominates your behavior, while others may also be present to a lesser extent. To get an objective view, ask friends and family, or search for 'TA Drivers' online and use a questionnaire.

It's easy to see how some combinations of behaviors may come together in one package – for instance *Be Perfect* may be common in those who also *Try Hard*. It's also easy to see how some combinations might be particularly destructive together – for instance *Being Strong* and *Please me/others* can be harmful to someone who's shouldering a lot of burden for the sake of others, while discounting their own needs.

It's also possible to undermine your own performance by not being aware of an unfortunate combination. *Be Perfect* and *Hurry Up* together are unlikely to yield the quality of work that you or anyone else regards as perfect. You can see how it's easy to undermine your own and everyone else's expectations without realizing.

My advice, like in the previous strategies, is to get a good fix on your own default mode of operation. See if you can recognize the drivers in your team and help them become aware of unhelpful behavior, resulting from *their* drivers. For example, if someone is always impatient in meetings and skims over difficult issues, perhaps they have to reign in a strong *Hurry Up* driver. Rushing others is not particularly engaging and almost always comes across as self-interested. They might be advised to park their agenda more often and try listening more.

Another way to use this is to **assemble teams of people who share the drivers that you need**. If you require a lot of independent work, perhaps find someone who values *Be Strong*. If you, as the manager of the team, have this trait, then learn to seek help and input where you're weak.

Though TA Drivers pull us towards mental goals or values, much of what we do – at a hygiene level – can be explained by looking through the lens of loss aversion. The loss of an opportunity, loss of face, money, status, or the loss of a perceived advantage or gain are fundamental to just about every choice we ever make. There are riches to be gained by betting that each of us is continuously driven to avoid future regret.

Questions

1. My TA Drivers: ....
2. Adverse impact this has on me and others: ....
3. My actions and support needed to recognize and manage those drivers: ....
4. Combination of my TA Drivers with my Operating Modes and Parent Adult Child (e.g. Please Others/ Carer/ Adaptive Child or Be Strong/ Controller/ Protective Parent): ....

Strategy #7: Are Limiting Beliefs in Your Way?

Okay, so you're beginning to understand how you and others behave and interact.

It's time to challenge what you believe, because, *believe* it or not, you're *still* getting in the way of your own success. In a sense, overcoming that single issue is what this much of this book is about.

We seem wired to defeat ourselves and sabotage our impact in a multitude of ways.

Sometimes, for example, fearing certain failure, we don't reach far enough to overcome difficult hurdles. We're also socially conditioned to stop short on something when we're not certain about the outcome for ourselves and for others. This is a caretaker mentality and pulls strongly on our strong loss aversion. It means we proceed *little* on what we want *a lot* of the time.

So, do you know how your beliefs work against you? And how would you know? Do you even know what you believe?

The Belief Cycle

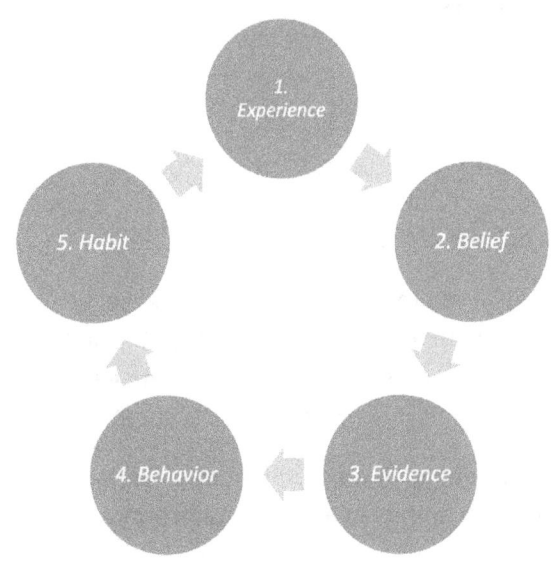

Take a look at how beliefs form:

1. You have experiences – good and bad. For example, I tried X but I did badly. In the language of TA Drivers, I like to *Be Perfect* and X was far from it
2. You form a belief based on the evidence. Y is normally the poor result whenever I try X
3. You seek out confirming evidence for your beliefs – A and B agree that I'm not good at X and avoid evidence that disproves your beliefs – it wasn't all bad, I'm a beginner and A/B don't know the whole story (but I'll ignore that because I have a belief to

protect). This is something called the ladder of inference at work (more on that later) and the result is that you start to become entrenched in your unhelpful beliefs

4. You begin to behave consistently with your beliefs. Every action reinforces the belief as you begin to avoid repeating your experience (and avoid disproving it). You avoid X and chastise yourself. Congratulations, you've now created a self-reinforcing habitual way of thinking that isn't productive or helpful
5. Your brain re-wires itself accordingly to cement this way of thinking from repeated experience. You spend an entire lifetime with the belief, flogging a dead horse is easier than trying to gain some perspective. Changing your view now entails a *loss to you* – after all, you don't want to have been wrong all those years!
6. An eon has passed and you've changed, along with the world. You now have a new experience of X and *it wasn't as bad as you expected.* But you think you just got lucky. It's now become impossible to shift your belief because you brain is incredibly slow at re-wiring. It takes a lot of mental effort, so you just find it easier to live with your limiting belief about yourself.

You can see how experience is the seed of belief, and how a limited perspective can generate and reinforce unhelpful beliefs.

Unless new experiences come along – frequently and consistently – you'll find yourself stuck in old beliefs, behaviors and habits. Going back up the chain is hard work and a slow process.

The best ways I've found, to avoid this limiting belief trap, are in understanding the competence cycle (you're not going to be good at anything right off the bat), diverse new experiences, challenging your assumptions and creating options which eliminate your attachment to a consistent way of thinking.

As an example, one of my team – a Promoter type – disliked detailed analysis. He had a particular aversion to working with spreadsheets, though they were becoming a bigger part of his role. Over the years, he had somehow decided that he didn't do spreadsheets and frequently delegated them to others within his teams. Though a perfectly sound strategy, it also left him with an Achilles heel as he slowly reinforced his own belief that he didn't do spreadsheets. The remedy was quick and easy – he just got on with them (new experience), stumbled a few times (competence cycle) and found he wasn't so bad after all (challenged his assumptions). He became less and less tense when faced with details analysis over time (new beliefs). Though this is not a big story, it's an extremely common scenario in many offices.

Inherent in belief forming is a tendency towards myopia – we quickly begin to treat the possibilities that we've closed out as if they are not there at all.

At first, you might not believe what you see as the result of your new experience; seeing, as the saying goes, is ultimately believing, so persist with new experiences.

It's not hard to see then that we are totally made by what we are involved in and what we experience daily – what we see, what we read, what we do and the people who influence us. The key to change is new experience.

But how does all this help with impact? As your challenges grow, you'll come up against your own limitations more frequently. You need to learn to get out of your own way. Here's the process for tackling limiting beliefs:

1) We've already read that experience is key. You have to change your experience and dive into a new one as quickly as possible. Don't try to think your way out of a limiting belief – it's virtually impossible, because you now know that you probably have a narrow point of view to start off with
2) Start immediately and start small. Remember that you may be somewhat incompetent at something new and things may feel difficult at first. That's the norm in the beginning of anything
3) Ensure that your new experiences are consistent and frequent. Your brain will pay attention to repeated signals and begin to re-wire itself accordingly. New beliefs will begin to form and things will get easier
4) Evidence is also key. When you read the ladder of inference below, you will know to gather and acknowledge new evidence to challenge the assumptions and beliefs you may have had in the

past. Don't just look for evidence that reinforces what you already think.

You can use this approach to influence and change others too.

The best product companies do this all the time. As an example, Apple tends to incorporate features into their products early to create experiences, so that when people really need to change two or three years down the line, they already believe that it's actually possible. A good example is Apple's Siri voice assistant, which – years after its launch – became a key way to interact with Apple's first smartwatch product.

Questions

1. How will I recognize a limiting belief at play (e.g. certain situations, mentoring or feedback)? ....
2. What assumptions or experiences lie beneath the limiting beliefs? ....
3. How I will challenge and test the assumptions in small ways? ....
4. What regular new experiences will I create in order to form new beliefs? ....

Strategy #8: Driving with the Brakes On

Like limiting beliefs, living with your inbuilt biases is like driving with the brakes on – you're still moving, but you just don't realize just how slowly you're going because it's always been that way.

Wikipedia lists dozens of baked-in biases, but look at the diagram below for some of the most significant ones.

Unhelpful Biases

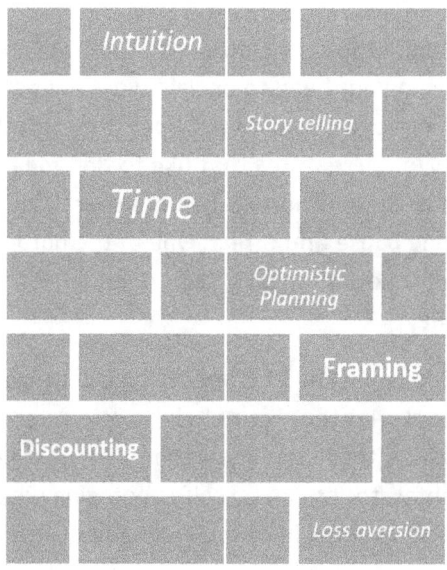

Intuition: Humans are good at intuiting – basically **making assumptions and rules of thumb based on past experience.** We love to trust our intuition because it's easy. Machines, on the other hand, are good at calculating and processing lots of data in real time. These two strengths are complimentary but seemingly not interchangeable. What you may not realise, however, is that **intuition is really just small-time calculation.** It's simply the process of adding up a limited set of past experiences to project a future. The more experience you have, therefore, the better your intuition may be. However, be careful because the opposite is also true and less experience often leads to over-confidence in our intuition. This is the ladder of inference at work and we'll talk about that soon.

Tip: When you do need to tell stories to get something, go to someone who relies on intuition.

Story-telling: When the shit hits the fan, do you create a narrative in your head to explain what happened and what's going to happen next? I'll bet you can't stop yourself. **We're creatures that like to find meaning even where there is none, or where there's no directly attributable cause and effect.** One of the hardest things for humans to do is to just accept randomness as the norm in life.

The downside of story-telling is that we get trapped in stories that are unhelpful. We dwell on them and this takes its toll on time and mental energy. Worst of all, mental stories can be self-sabotaging when things go wrong and we begin to see inevitability inside a predicament. It's as if we talk ourselves into adversity. Sometimes, things just don't work out. No story.

The best performers, however, learn to act on first instinct to avoid this trap. That is to say, 'What can I do now with whatever I have? What's my very next step?' You'll see sports champions operate in this way each time they play. They ignore their second instinct to rationalize and personalize what just went wrong when they lose a point. Instead they laser focus on what to do in the very next step.

Time: It has been said that the when time was invented, humanity's problems began. We're trained from an early age to be a slave to time, to march to the drumbeat of the world. But this means we continuously project into an imagined future or dwell on images from the past. And because we can't deal with imagined crises in the future or unresolved problems in the past, thinking about them sets up an anxiety gap. Your head wants to act, but your body can't do anything in the past or future, and this thought process can be crippling.

Powerful performers learn to be present and simply work with whatever is in front of them now. It's as if the future adds up to nothing more than a stack of all the present moments. This is called Presence and to remain present, regularly take 30 seconds to mentally and deliberately close off distractions – prior engagements, discussions, meetings and expectations – put them into an imaginary box for later and shut the lid, then focus on the immediate task at hand.

Optimistic Planning: We routinely **underestimate the time, effort and resource to do almost anything**, even when we've done the same thing a hundred times over. Part of this is cultural in corporate life – we tend to shoot whistleblowers and bearers of unwanted news.

We're also just as buoyed by heroic struggles, even if they are hopeless. This is because they suggest grit, determination and the right stuff. It's beneficial to be wired this way – to be on the front foot – otherwise we'd talk ourselves out of everything before ever starting. Have you ever thought *If only I knew what this would take, I might never have started*? I'm certain that that can be said for every significant human endeavor in history.

A big part of this bias is myopia – we simply don't see the obstacles that are off-stage and we're derailed by challenges that we never saw coming.

The best ways to overcome these biases are to manage downside risks for times when things could go wrong. This is a way to avoid shooting yourself in the foot over something which could easily have been mitigated. You can also add an appropriate buffer to soak up problems, for example 30-50% contingency on your worst case, whether money or time. It's often best to squirrel away this buffer so it's not at the mercy of the planning fallacy of others.

Loss aversion: Have you ever noticed how it takes effort to be positive? Whereas the negative seems to take care of itself? It seems we are made to fear loss, and while loss aversion is a great motivator, it also means

we spend a lot of time worrying about imagined loss without realizing it – whether control, money, relationships, or even death.

When loss becomes a habitual way of experiencing the world – by virtue of your job, perhaps as a *Caretaker* who has to keep everything under *Perfect* control – it can eventually lead to persistent and unhelpful beliefs and result in chronic stress. This bias leaves many people living with an underlying low-grade anxiety, but the best way to avoid this is to have consistent and persistent positive experiences, even if you have to manufacture them – for instance simply acknowledging the upside in events – however deluding that might initially seem in adverse situations (we explore being grateful in Volume 2). We induce positive experiences through stories too, so perhaps consume more of things you like.

Some people say a ratio of 5 Positive to 1 Negative is an evenly balanced ratio!

But it's also invaluable to see how loss aversion affects those around you each day so you can anticipate their moves. As an example, later in careers, people seem to play defensively and protect what they've built over the years. Early in careers there's less to lose, so people take more risks without them appearing so *risky*. How someone makes a choice depends on their starting point then subconsciously they ask themselves if they'll gain or lose by virtue of where they're starting from. In simple terms:

a) If someone has something or all to *lose* you should bet on them first walking away. People will avoid triggering a loss and will even take irrational risks to avoid it. At the extreme, loss avoidance feels like a gain, epitomized by the phrase 'nothing left to lose' if I take this bacon saving action
b) If they see only *gain* you should bet on them going for it. People will avoid any risk of losing a gain (it switches to a potential loss). The initial stage is epitomized by the phrases 'only upside' or 'nothing to lose', the latter by 'everything to lose'

Companies and individuals behave in a similar manner. Companies facing near certain bankruptcy tend to make poor decisions and often cut prices to the bone to shed inventory or gain market share. This is usually an effort to save themselves and is an example of taking risk to avoid a loss (saving their bacon). Conversely, companies which are comfortable in the status quo often don't see or acknowledge the next innovation, let alone take advantage of it. This is an example of avoiding risk to a currently favorable position. And it's the Young Turks that often take the leap and come to eat their lunch.

Understanding and taming your loss aversion will also have a big influence on your risk tolerance. Think of your aversion as a dial in your subconscious – its main aim is to protect you from danger and loss. By challenging assumptions and projections inside your head, you can learn to be much more tolerant of risk, taking calculated steps to mitigate downsides. That said, it's also necessary to have good process and appropriate focus to manage risk effectively. More of that in Volume 2.

Framing: The way a discussion, argument, or anything is presented – or framed – determines our starting point and the way things will proceed.

One obvious example of this is the classic: *start high* in a price negotiation, with the expectation that price will move *downwards* (also known as an anchor). The negotiation has been framed to move in a certain way.

We're all familiar with the phrase *lies, damned lies and statistics*. What this points to is the reality that numbers can be fudged to present any picture one wants to give. A common example is a price chart – the rise or fall over a period can be made to look visually significant just by changing the scale on the vertical axis. This is the most common framing we live with daily and without necessarily noticing.

Combining framing and loss aversion is a surprisingly powerful way of moving others to act. Any event can be made to look like a loss or a gain, depending on how you frame it (think of a glass half empty or half full). It's the same glass, but framed as a gain or a loss.

What you see here are dopamine (gain) and cortisol (loss) in action – the only two reasons any of us ever get out of bed (caffeine, nicotine and other drugs aside). Every moment of every life is virtually guaranteed to be underpinned by one or the other.

Knowing that people jump on gains and avoid losses, simply pitch or frame your requests as gains. You can also light a fire by threatening a loss (take a look at motivation above to understand what moves people).

We'll cover that more under motivation later on.

You can further enhance framing to your advantage with a technique called *suspending disbelief* from story-telling.

With this technique, you:

- Provide sufficient *real* detail to a picture to give the illusion of authenticity. For example: Britain joining the Eurozone is a bad idea – here are the supporting views of five people we talked to. You would then omit to mention the millions of Brits you didn't consult, who may have had a different opinion
- Provide an emotional hook or attachment, which would naturally have your audience voting for the outcome you want. In the example above, you could highlight a loss of sovereignty for Britain in the Eurozone, knowing that it would be hard for your audience to vote against, whatever they may believe about the Euro. Essentially you're trying to align your hook to people's general sense of what's right. For instance, stories about underdogs are powerful

because we always want underdogs to succeed – this means we're prepared to suspend our disbelief and judgment in order to permit the story to work.

You've been framed!

The best way to avoid framing, however, is to **challenge whether the issue, problem or discussion is starting from the right place in the first place**. Because we all tend to ignore information that's off-stage, there's always a good chance that it hasn't.

Discounting: We talked about discounting in the example above. It is when someone **overlooks or avoids what they don't understand, as if it doesn't matter.** What can you do? Invite challenge and incorporate diverse views in your work, accepting that you can't see everything.

The upshot here is to beware of your biases at work under the radar. What do you automatically like or dislike, revere or fear without question? How do you react on autopilot? Those are the things that'll hold you back when you should be moving full steam ahead.

Questions

1. The key biases I fall for without realizing: ....

2. When they tend to occur and how I will mitigate them: .

3. Alignment to my operating modes or drivers e.g. insufficient *Analysis* by a *Promoter* who also tends to *Hurry Up*: ....

Strategy #9: Sprinkle on Some Gestalt

> Gestalt: '...our ability to acquire and maintain meaningful perceptions in an apparently chaotic world.' Wikipedia

Another way of saying this is that we find meaning in disparate elements that may have no real connection.

We are story-telling creatures and experts at creating meaning even when, objectively, it's absent. And it is Gestalt which gives rise to our need for closure and symmetry. It's as though we're compelled to shine a light on darkness. Take a look at the dark shapes below:

Nothing but a Few Dark Shapes Here

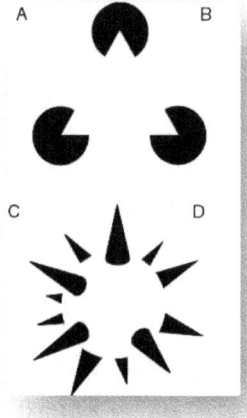

Did you see the disconnected dark shapes? Hands up if you believe you saw some light shapes too. Now look at the shapes again and try to disbelieve completely that you saw any light shapes (I'm being deliberately vague here to avoid framing you). It's impossible, isn't it?

So how does Gestalt drive and, more importantly, derail us?

- We infer grand intent from behavior, even though we can't read minds
- We reverse cause for effect to satisfy what we want to see, even if there's no causality
- We hold visions of the future, even though key components of the vision are missing today

- We prefer symmetrical charts and even intervals, although these may be overly simplistic
- We compulsively tick off to-dos to find satisfaction, even if they're not worth doing
- We stop the clock prematurely on something difficult, just to feel like we're done
- We naturally assume the role of Parent to someone who's acting the Child
- Our stories need resolution, so we make them up, even without requisite information.

Gestalt compels us to seek closure even when things aren't complete and that gap drives incessant thought and busy minds. It compels us to find stories and patterns where there are none of any significance.

When combined with the *Hurry Up* TA Driver trait you can see how Gestalt can derail you into taking premature action and decisions, or to arrive at conclusions with inadequate information. The answer is to loosen your grip on the need for closure and sometimes allow things to run their course in their own time.

So, given its power, how can you create Gestalt (satisfaction, vision, inspiration and fantasy) in others? And, vitally, how do you prevent *yourself* being Gestalted unsuspectingly into Cloud Cuckoo Land?

The tool of choice for the former is good story-telling. The most effective framework I know for preventing the latter is the Ladder of Inference or Judgement – that's up next.

When it comes to stories, you can find more satisfaction in your work by simply telling yourself favorable stories. It may sound phony, but remember that your sub-conscious can't necessarily tell the difference between reality and fantasy. Consider also that you listen to – and buy stories – from all around, every minute of every day from the second you're born. Just create your own. In fact, whether you realize it or not, you're already doing just that. Simply pick the good ones.

Gestalt can be a good thing – in fact there's little point judging it, because it's simply a part of us. Look for Gestalt (satisfaction) in the mere doing of whatever it is that you do, instead of the achievement of some future fantasy outcome. The doing is obviously the only way of achieving any outcome in any case and of getting an extra shot of Gestalt with it. That's presence in a nutshell, too.

When we look at making good decisions in Volume 2, we'll look at the role of Gestalt in driving us to choose prematurely and make poor decisions – all for the sake of ticking things off a list.

Questions

1. When do you buy or create stories which aren't necessarily there (think of loss of vision situations)? ....
2. How do these stories derail your energy and confidence?
3. What can you do more of to find Gestalt or satisfaction? .
4. Where can you use stories to create Gestalt for others? ..

Strategy #10: Ladder of Inference (or Judgment)

We form judgments and beliefs about *everything*, based on the information available. Sometimes we have enough and our judgments are sound, but a lot of times we have too little, and our judgments may also be unreliable.

In his life-changing book *Thinking, Fast and Slow* author Daniel Kahneman suggests that **we readily and easily form beliefs about the world, even when we have inadequate information to create a good picture**. It seems that we're built to ignore what we don't know or understand and then to substitute the void with proxies or assumptions. These are rules of thumb or heuristics, and they appear in our sub-conscious without our awareness.

Why do we shoot ourselves in the foot like this? Well, it's simply easier to form conclusions out of assumptions, rather than wait for missing information that we may never get. Brains are also lazy and chasing new information takes work and effort.

Furthermore, **we sub-consciously seek out information that corroborates our beliefs, desires and assumptions once they have formed**. It's as if we're attached to being right and feel compelled to prove ourselves. If you think that's bad, it gets worse. At the same time, we shun information (even legitimate information) that doesn't conform to our views. This thinking pattern reinforces itself and our beliefs become hard wired, whatever they are, as we age. You can read more about in Limiting Beliefs above.

If this all sounds far-fetched, consider the popular phrase *lies, damned lies and statistics* once again. Most people realize quickly that analysis in the business world is often a mechanism for supporting a pre-existing point of view or an agenda. Most business analysis, or sales and marketing material, present a picture that supports a product or service and almost always avoids showing opposing perspectives. Shooting yourself in the foot just doesn't sell.

When you build a pitch, for instance, you might scour archives for information that helps the case, but you're unlikely to uphold information which opposes what you're trying to sell, even if it's legitimate. Take, for example, something known as a *benefits statement;* a common business tool for supporting business change. These are perfectly designed to talk ourselves and others into doing something, but rarely, if ever, espouse differing views. It would seem unnatural to do so.

We're extraordinarily adept at discounting information we simply don't understand, but plough on regardless, making poor choices as we go. Consider financial service products like insurance and pensions. Complexity has become the tool of choice, because it's easier to befuddle someone into a poor choice than explain the details, then risk them walking away. Have you ever tried to make sense of a pension statement or read the small print in an insurance document? Do you routinely put the brakes on when you don't understand something, or simply continue regardless? Most people continue with financial affairs regardless.

In a nutshell, **we readily jump to conclusions and make assumptions when we don't have information.** Why? Well, it would be exhausting and paralyzing to challenge everything we think and believe all the time.

The Ladder of Inference – Do Look Down

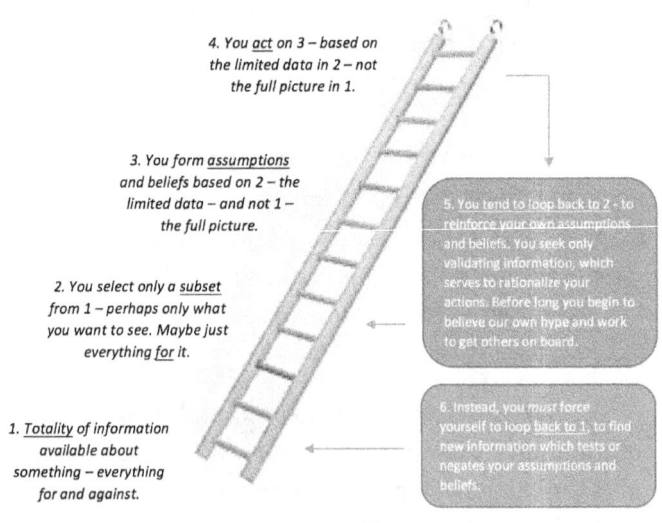

Stage 1

Every situation arrives with actual information about what's happening.

For example, if we're looking to buy stock, we could begin by looking at how the overall market for a class of investments or a particular manager has performed. What we'd get here is unbiased actual performance information. Often, however, this is too much to process, or we simply don't understand some of the information we are looking at, so we tend to jump straight to Stage 2 as quickly as humanly possible. Industries such as financial services are expert at driving us to stage 2 quickly, though we naturally do this by ourselves too.

Stage 2

We almost always go with a subset of information – that which grabs our attention – even if this isn't the full picture. At this point we've only looked at what we recognized or wanted to see – not the whole picture. Stage 2 is a position of early bias.

As an example, stage 2 information may be represented by the broker's sales brochure, which is unlikely to show performance shortfalls or significant risks. It may have simple pictures and descriptions, suitable for ten-year olds, avoiding anything which might invoke mental challenge. It may look coherent and sufficiently glossy and we may be short of time or attention, so we jump to stage 3.

Meanwhile the full picture in stage 1 may have shown us tanking performance over the last decade.

Stage 3

We felt comfortable enough in stage 2, to now form assumptions and beliefs. We believe the salesman knows his business and the investment performs, from the data we've seen.

We now have *forming ideas* and evidence – the sales brochure – to confirm them. So, we feel comfortable to act and sign on the line to buy the broker's services.

Stage 4

We now act on the forming ideas and sign on the line. This ensures that we act consistently with our beliefs in stage 3, and appear rational to ourselves and others around us.

Stage 5

To check we did the right thing, signing on the dotted line, we loop back to the data for more information. But we normally only go back to stage 2 – the limited data set to hand, or that which we understand.

This way, we end up rationalizing our beliefs or actions because we want to look coherent and right. We still feel comfortable, so we're now unwilling to challenge our original beliefs or assumptions – which were made on limited or flawed data.

Stage 6

The key, then, to making better choices and decisions, is to go back to stage 1, and test that we had the full picture from a range of sources – and not just corroborating information in stage 2.

In stage 2, we also need to ensure we select a wide range of information and not just what we want to see, hear, believe or understand. If we don't understand something, we call in expert input before deciding to ignore it.

So, **try to stop yourself making assumptions without any real backing or with a limited point of view**. Push yourself to see the world through different eyes and not just your own to get a full picture. Realize that everyone arrives at a challenge with a different set of experiences, filters and back stories. Then have the courage to invite independent views to challenge your own beliefs and make sure to listen rather than defend. The best time to do this is usually early on, before you and everyone else becomes set in their opinions and egos are at stake. Earlier is always easier – you don't want to invest a lot of time in something that wasn't going to work from the outset.

On the flip side, you can also use this principle to thwart ideas that you don't like. Earlier in the process is easier, but leaving it late in the cycle will make something you don't want harder to unwind.

In summary, here's the key ways to avoid the ladder of judgment:

- Incorporate diversity in your teams. Aim for different but constructive view points
- Test assumptions and beliefs and hold them loosely
- Catch yourself if you're looking only at corroborating information, or talking only to the likeminded
- Adapt quickly to new information
- Practice listening and not just telling
- Be suspect of any claims of benefits without an adequate exploration of downsides
- Be particularly wary of the ladder when you're a novice, because a novice *always* acts as an incompetent without realizing. We are also most vulnerable to limited data when we are uncertain how to behave or progress – so we look to others who are confirming, perhaps making the same mistakes
- But be wary too when you're the expert – a firmly held view over a long period can be incredibly entrenching and will be wrong at times
- Don't allow first impressions to dominate. You're almost certain to be looking at a façade or unrepresentative picture whenever you do. Remember, that first impressions normally arise at the furthest psychic distance (see relationships above).
- The ladder is a mechanism for getting trapped in our own negative thoughts. Rather than sweep them under the carpet, learn to challenge the assumptions and stories behind them – stories that aren't actually there until we conjure them up.

What's interesting is how the Ladder of Judgment can be combined with TA Drivers and Parent Adult Child to form a more complete picture of you (look back at those strategies as a reminder if you need to).

At one extreme, you might be fiercely independent (maybe a Be Strong tendency) and form your assumptions and judgments alone with limited or no input. There's a danger here of being stuck in your own world view and finding yourself trying to force it through, come what may.

You might have the worldview of 'I'm okay – You're not okay'. When you take on a Parent position over others, you might find yourself assuming that others are slow and wishing they would 'Hurry Up' frequently too. You might have to slow down to see if they're dwelling on something important for a reason that you've not seen.

At the opposite extreme, you might take the worldview that 'I'm not okay' and find yourself dwelling on one criticism over your work, while ignoring all the good work you've also done. This is surprisingly common for Be Perfect types and is an example of selecting limited data and reinforcing flawed beliefs.

As you can see, there isn't necessarily a single prescriptive combination of factors, so self-awareness is key here. That awareness allows you to make an informed choice over your behavior and decisions.

Questions

1. Where and when do you limit input to protect your own assumptions and beliefs? ....
2. How might that arise from your operating modes and drivers? ....
3. How will you act to avoid the ladder of inference? ....
4. Where can you use stories to create Gestalt for others? ..

Strategy #11: Step Outside Your Comfort Zone – About 4% Out Should Do It – and Get Creative

What is the comfort zone? A nice mattress and soft pillows? And how do you get out of it? Walk to the shower?

The Bell Curve or 80:20 of Genius

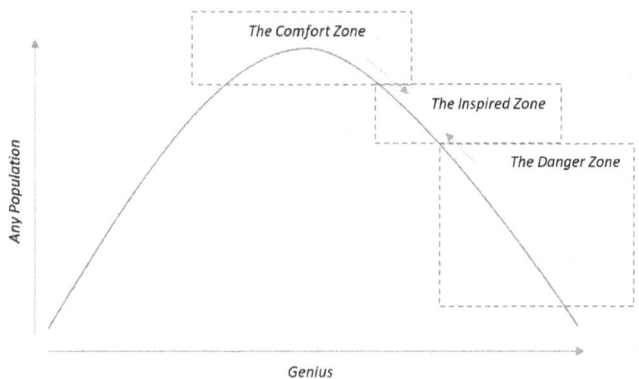

The Dreaded Comfort Zone

The chart shows that when we talk about a comfort zone, it generally means sitting inside a pool of average people in any population, which may be the office, a company, the country or so on. We all tend to believe that we're above average in abilities, without realizing that that's in fact a perfectly average point of view.

We tend to like living in the comfort zone and we even seem pre-disposed to it. As soon as we settle into a steady income, we begin to mow the lawn at the weekends and take 2.5 holidays per year, get an SUV and begin to enjoy taking a dog for a walk.

Our idea of creativity is buying the next iteration of smartphone or re-decorating the bathroom. It does in fact sound quite average, does it not?

So, you've now decided to get out of your comfort zone; but if you do, beware of...

The Danger Zone

Your ideas are now unleashed and everyone thinks you're barmy. You think about changing the world, of revolution, but your ideas seem extreme and stray into fantasy. Conventions were established for good reason, but you've defied, ignored or jeered at them, so no one gets you and you fail to engage others. You may well end up biting an ear off – alone, of course. Someone, somewhere might discover your ideas, some day.

The downside to creativity is that no one sees genius coming, because it can look like madness to the average populous. What's more, few can or are willing to stray too far outside of their own comfort zone for the sake of another's ideas. Why? Monthly payments, reputations and relationships are at stake and these all rely on things remaining more or less as they are.

If you know anything about the making of *Star Wars*, for example, you'll know just how traumatic an experience it was for George Lucas. Nobody (not even he himself) expected anything but a flop at the box office and Lucas even fled to Hawaii to avoid the embarrassment of opening night. Because there was nothing quite like it at the time, to most, including the cast, it looked like madness in the making. But Lucas, of course, made the most of story convention – The Hero's Journey and story arcs, for example – and revolutionized cinema. To do that, he collected battle scars and deep wounds from his madness (he had a breakdown in hospital). That's how genius often starts. Aside from one other genius, no one thought he was a genius, until the results came in. That other genius was Steven Spielberg.

So, if you find that you have *no* scars from whatever it is you are doing, it may be a sure sign that you're swimming around in mediocrity. The desire for comfort and avoidance of struggle is the single biggest reason why the world's chock full of evolution and only talk of revolution.

As Lucas demonstrated, creative ideas inside the danger zone are risky and best avoided in the office or in the mainstream commercial world. They have a high risk of failure and disillusionment – if they involve others (ahem, everything involves others) – and you open yourself up to chronic low-level stress. Humans are poor at handling chronic stress and eventually burnout. But that shouldn't bother you if you really want to change the world, because luckily, there's the...

The Inspired Zone

This is the zone of creative evolution, not revolution. 4% outside of your comfort zone – give or take. It's safe for the Averages to step into this zone because it's just a short walk back home if it all gets too uncomfortable.

If you look around at any consumer product, for instance, you'll see that virtually all of them evolve within this realm of creativity – whether new cars, movies or liquid soaps. In essence, all this zone requires is re-packaging of old ideas into new combinations. If you can remember the following adages that capture this, you're on the right track and it will be much easier to take others with you and implement your creative ideas step by step, rather than leap by leap:

- The same, but better, e.g. annual technology upgrades, super hero movies;

- We all stand on the shoulders of giants, e.g. tablet computers (or glorified smartphones).

You may get a shot of acute stress every now and then when things don't work out, but short acute stress fades quickly and is even thought to be a good thing in any case.

Creativity is explored in depth in Volume 2.

Questions

1. If you often find yourself out on a limb or your ideas are misunderstood, how can you reel in your fantasies to make them more practical and engaging? ....

2. If you only live in comfort, how can you take tiny steps into something useful, new and uncomfortable? ....

Strategy #12: Avoid What You're Not Cut Out For

Okay, now that we've explored motivation in depth, and understood how fundamental it is to impact, here's a strategy to help you think about whether you're in the right place for you – and if not, how you can clear the path to being the best you can be. We'll get slightly esoteric for a few strategies.

I'm going to make a big assumption here – that you're satisfied in your current role – however, you'd stop what you're working on and dance on the tabletop at the drop of a lottery check. Are you really sure you're satisfied?

Why do I ask? Because doing what motivates you is presence 101. You want presence, don't you? If you can't move to do what you want, you won't find presence. If you don't find presence, your impact will be much diminished.

Operating this way, you'll reach your own invisible ceiling without necessarily knowing why. You'll be the one waiting to clock out each day.

That isn't exceptional – it's the average human condition. You may, in all probability, do well enough for a while, but you'll eventually fizzle out, sabotage your own success and get frustrated.

Others, who'd love to have your job will put in the hours required to get it and then get really good at it too. If you're not willing to match that, you will always feel mediocre and threatened.

Conversely, when you're in your zone, **an invisible energy fuels you** like nothing else and that propels you from strength to strength.

So, **focus your energies on leveraging your strengths and delegate your weaknesses if you're in a position to do so**. Focus on what you're good at, the things that are most important to your job, and get noticed by those in power.

A good manager, for instance, knows how to delegate to a team all the things that he or she isn't personally good at. This is a way of thinking and focusing, which is essential to *all* success and impact.

When passion for what you're doing is present, it shines through with its own energy. You won't need so much strength to go where others naturally fear to tread. Some people call it finding your purpose.

But don't take anyone else's word for it – there's a lot of manufactured passion out there – simply to reel in resource for things which are simply not deserving.

Question

1. What do you do right now that you really ought to delegate or outsource? ....

Strategy #13: Work Somewhere You Like

Okay, let's say you *chose* to bite the bullet. You realised you were in the wrong place and that you'd never top the charts or have genuine sustainable impact.

You couldn't put in enough energy to stand out.

You stopped short at obstacles and hurdles that separated you from those who succeeded, even though you thought, averagely, that you were *above* average.

Realize that whatever your goal or dream, you'll spend 99% of your time clawing your way towards it – and not standing at the end of the rainbow – assuming that you do get *there* eventually. That 99% of your time has to be worth it, because the end of the journey may not be all it's cracked up to be.

Furthermore, when you get *there* – wherever *there* is – you may not even notice. Have you noticed, instead, how your mind is always on the next thing and the next thing, and so on? The chances are that you won't even stop to notice the flowers when you arrive at your rose garden. This is particularly likely if you're ambitious and driven in the first place.

So, focus on the experience – how you spend your time – and not necessarily on the outcomes, which you or anyone can dream up.

Questions

1. Are you outcome driven? ....

2. How does that impact your enjoyment of what you do e.g. you don't stop to smell the roses? ....

3. How will you acknowledge the joy of what you *do* more, whatever the outcome? ....

Strategy #14: *The Force* Won't Help You

You may believe that simply wanting something invokes a mystical force across the universe to begin lining up the stars for you. Maybe – but what about the 7 billion other people who also want something? It's pretty self-evident that you don't find 7 billion people with whatever they want.

Still, there's always hope.

Impactful people don't rely on hope – they focus on what they control. And now, having argued for your freedom of choice, there's clearly a limit to what you can personally control.

We spend all day simply coming up against all the choices that everyone else has too – different choices, usually, to ours. Nothing nefarious necessarily – just people pulling in their own direction. And that's the real paradox of choice – it's essentially unconstrained, yet limited at the same time.

And some people can push their choices along further and faster than we can. And that's the problem.

So, here's the thing – only make choices that you have control over.

So much anguish, disappointment and lamenting is poured over what we don't control.

Having a project dumped on you may not be your choice, but you can choose to do whatever is required to get it done and out of the way. This is a choice that you have.

Getting a raise or promotion may not be in your control, but focusing instead on trying to be the right person for your job, is in your control.

Let go of what you don't control, because if you can't control it, then why worry about it?

Equally, if you can control something, then why worry about it?

Is there anything left to lament?

In summary, make good choices over what you do control and nothing else.

Questions

1. How will you catch yourself if you're becoming despondent over what you don't control? ....

2. How will you change the story in your head from *should*, to *not in my control*? ....

3. How will you redirect your attention to impact what you do control? ....

Strategy #15: Get a Coach or a Mentor

There's a common perception that to get the best out of people, you simply understand their preferences and put them there. For instance, it makes good sense to label a quant jock as the Spreadsheet Manager and not as the People Manager. That all makes sense and goes some distance, but it's only fine for cogs who will never be anything else.

People, of course, are not cogs. They almost always have undiscovered potential for one simple reason: they often avoid stepping out of their preference and comfort zone – because it hurts to do so.

We in fact encourage people to stick to what they already know by piling on them what they're already good at. So, it takes a skilled coach or mentor – and sometimes the stick too – to really drive people to achieve all that they can.

Don't get me wrong, this isn't about duress or squeezing out the last drop, or even pushing people around. So, why is this necessary?

As you've read, it takes a remarkable amount of self-awareness to know the imagined limitations that you put in your own way. But even then, your awareness of the limitations is incomplete, because the subconscious and conscious are not wired 1-to-1. We're simply *designed* to be incapable of perceiving much of what goes on below the surface – even though that's the source of all our drive.

Think of loss aversion and all the biases we've talked about. All of these skew the world that you see and often make it look quite scary. That fear is only tamed with objectivity, knowledge and experienced support.

It takes a remarkable amount of self-control to push beyond these in-built limitations, because they are there to hold you back from imagined danger.

If you are a novice at something, you are in a state of unconscious incompetence. When you fail in the early stages of anything new, it can be disheartening. However, that's also the norm – it's called learning to walk.

The best way to avoid your own limitations is to invite outside views. For instance, enlist the help of a coach or someone you trust who has a different perspective to you; someone willing to save you from your own hype.

Understand that people can rarely if ever get the best out of themselves alone.

Think of a coach or mentor as an accountability partner.

Questions

1. Where are you frequently blindsided by inexperience or discomfort? ....

2. How might a coach or mentor help? ....

Strategy #16: Anxiety Attack!

I once walked out of an office with a colleague at the end of a long day – a long week – after a big meeting with our project Board. We'd had a pressured build up, trying to save our project from competing interests and skepticism. But we put on a powerful show in the meeting and gained approval for the next phase from all the Board members.

Nevertheless, my colleague looked glum afterwards as we walked away.

Tired, I thought.

As we exited the revolving doors at the end of the day, she revealed a curious phenomenon she'd observed many times before but never really understood. Rationally at least, she believed we were back in a good place – but *inside* the picture was different. She expressed a nagging anxiety that seemed entrenched and impossible to shift. No amount of logic and rational explanation would calm it and it felt like her *insides* knew something that *she* didn't. I could almost see the two states fighting for supremacy inside her head at the same time. She looked pre-occupied and distant.

I recognized her dichotomy instantly. The pervasive anxiety seemed familiar, so we began to unpick it over the next few days. You might recognize it as irrational fear, nausea, sickness, dry mouth, sweaty palms, uncontrollable shaking or shivering and so on.

It became obvious that – inside at least – it was all or nothing thinking for her. A successful pitch to the project Board was going to keep her and her team fed, and may even have determined her promotion prospects. Lose the project and she'd be walking back to the office in shame, given all the effort she and several people had put into winning it.

She was locked into winner takes all thinking and had ramped up the stakes so high that she wasn't sure she was up to the fight anymore. **It was as if the imaginary plank she'd been walking on the ground (quite safely) was now jacked up ten foot in the air – same plank with disastrous imagined consequences.**

So, how could she have understood why inner anxiety often persisted in the face of logic?

Challenging Work Anxieties

Are *it's* (amygdala's) projections real or absolute? What makes more sense (frontal cortex)?

Anxiety ⇄ Assumptions

What does *it* want (the amygdala)?

Anxiety lives in the amygdala, an older and automatic part of the brain compared to the frontal cortex which does all the thinking. The amygdala's job is to see that you're safe, but it's got a big problem in the world of work – it plays too safe. It raises the alarm even if no alarm is required – and there's no volume rocker. You can't even talk to it. It does the moaning and knows how to crowd out everything – especially if you've always allowed it a special seat in your head. It gives your frontal cortex fearful projections to act on, and if unchallenged, the frontal cortex accepts then validates them as if real (recall our propensity to loss aversion above). This becomes a self-reinforcing cycle and downward spiral at the extreme.

The first step for my colleague seemed to be to listen in and simply acknowledge her feeling of anxiety. Fighting or sweeping it under a rug was futile – her brain seemed to have an inbuilt immunity to mind control of any sort! Waves of anxiety returned over the subsequent days.

It helped her to label them specifically and write them down – she wrote that she felt *disheartened* – and observed them from a pretend camera suspended in the air looking inside her head. She imagined the epicenter of her anxiety to be the mid-brain which looked like the stub of her spine extending into her head. It's a small primitive part with no capacity to reason or think – its only job was to just react and keep her from imagined (or real) danger.

Her strategy was to **not judge it**, but just be curious of the feeling and accept it for what it was, asking 'what does *it* want?', as if it were a distinct and autonomous part of her. This strategy tamed the pressure needle at least 50%.

It seems that some people need calm to feel their best – others still, need to raise the stakes and apply a little pressure to turn up the fire. Which are you? Think back to when you were at your best.

Second, she began to draw out the assumptions and projections playing in her head – to test their validity. She took her assumptions to the extreme and made them seem ridiculous. She imagined security walking her off the client premises and out the door for not bringing in the project. She imagined her desk cleared back at the office – save for a severed horse head on the desktop. That's after her security pass was wiped clean. How likely were these outcomes? In place of her anxiety, she was soon laughing…

...because we all tend to focus on the negatives.

But she noted that it was important to respect the reasons behind her anxieties. The amygdala wouldn't be fooled easily. There was no sweeping under rugs or dismissive assumptions. The frontal cortex really had to think and act.

Third, she reframed her anxiety as excitement and used her nervous energy to pretend she was energized for the challenges ahead. She acknowledged the project was important to her, otherwise she would have felt indifferent.

Fourth, she stopped trying to control outcomes that her ego didn't control. When she was less desperate, she appeared less desperate. Instead she found presence in temporary distraction, allowing her anxiety to fade. The more she thought about negative outcomes, the more likely she would continue to think about negative outcomes (self-reinforcing pathways are created in the brain for whatever we think about repeatedly).

Finally, she decided to keep moving (physically), knowing that nothing entrenches anxiety like stillness.

Within days she had found a way to turn her nervous energy into positive action. Her attention focused back towards achieving the next (successful) project Board. Just one step at a time.

Questions

1. Do you get pre-occupied by anxieties at work when the stakes are high? ....

2. How does this impact your interactions with colleagues? ....

3. Does your track record suggest that you need calm or pressure to achieve your ambitions? ....

4. Which of the strategies above can help you tame your nerves? ....

Strategy #17: Manage Expectations and Don't Be High Maintenance

Ultimately, this is the key to survival in any job.

It means not over-promising, under-delivering, or constantly needing your hand holding.

Remember one thing – the quicker your respond to a request, from wherever, the easier it is to meet an expectation. The longer you wait, the more unlikely that becomes.

Expectations run rampant when you're not on top of them. If you procrastinate, your boss will already be halfway up the ladder of inference – when you're only just getting started.

But now you've understood his or her motivation (let's say fear from loss aversion), you know the dominating driver (Hurry Up), and you know the operating mode (Controller), and you know that the Child in him or her will appear and start throwing toys out the pram. You also know that you're a Promoter and don't normally pay sufficient attention to delivering, or that you're an Analyst and that you just need to do a little more to make sure everything lines up. You've read about relationships and now know that, as a doer, you would benefit from paying more attention to others. Whatever your, and your boss's, expectations – manage them.

Bosses prefer staff to whom they can off-load. They want to feel confident that the trash will be taken out to *their* expectations – even when it goes unsaid! If you're not a mind reader you'll need to remain highly proactive to stay on top of these expectations.

Your job is usually to make others in power – all along your career path – feel and look good in *their* own roles.

Some of these people in power may not be your boss – they may be part of your power network. If you're good, some of them will want to drag you up the ladder with them as they rise through the ranks.

In a sense, this is saying that you shouldn't give your full attention to your immediate boss, but reserve an adequate amount for your network.

Try to remember that influence is a numbers and options game and you'll see that your career is more likely to be determined by your network than your lowly boss alone.

So, let's repeat again – connect by understanding, and managing expectations.

Questions

1. Who in my network am I not attentive or responsive to and what will I do? ....

2. How will I better shape expectations before they run away without me? ....

Closing Remarks

I hope the strategies in this book have given you the tools for self-awareness, understanding behavior and motivation and for connecting to others – for big impact!

We've learnt powerful strategies to:

- **Figure out how we operate**: #1: Modes of Operation, #2: Parent, Adult and Child, #3 I'm Okay? Are You Okay?
- **Create the right relationships**: #4: Relationships are Everything
- **Understand our motivators, drivers and limiting beliefs**: #5: What Motivates You?, #6: What Drives You?, #7: Limiting Beliefs, #8: Driving with the Brakes On, #16: Anxiety Attack!
- **Understand and overcome natural tendencies and biases**: #9: Gestalt; #10: Ladder of Inference, #11: Comfort Zones
- **Avoid limiting choices**: #12: Avoid What You're Not Cut Out For, #13: Work Somewhere You Like, #14: The Force Won't Help You
- **Thrive and take it to the next level**: #15: Get a Coach or a Mentor, #17: Manage Expectations

Okay, now just go and practice these things! Only deliberate practice – and correcting your mistakes – makes perfect.

I hope you've learnt that simply showing up at work and quietly doing the external stuff in your job to the best of your ability is the least of your challenges for creating big impact. Those climbing the ladder will be throwing all of the above – and more – at you, whether or not you are aware that it is happening.

Remember also that learning is doing, not just reading or memorizing. Take one strategy at a time and make it part of your habit or routine. Incorporate another when the previous one's under your belt. Finally, dip back in and find something new on another commute, as you progress.

I'm confident that the material will be life changing if you systematically incorporate it into your life, because I've seen that in everyone I've coached.

This series is certain to benefit others, so don't hold back – share the strategies, whether in the office or at home, and help others get on track.

Talk to your boss, mentors, coaches, colleagues, family, or friends, and ask them to help you build an objective picture of *you* – from their perspective.

Please also be sure to review the book – describing how it helped you – on Amazon, iBooks, Kobo, or wherever you purchased it. That helps others to discover it and also provides feedback for future improvements.

Finally, if you want to join a training program based on the content of this book, or if you require coaching, or even if you just want more impact strategies, look for other books in the series at <u>60strategies.com</u> or follow the links in the front of this book.

Good luck, and let me know how you are doing via the series' website, at 60strategies.com.

You're now ready to discover how the best achieve extraordinary goals

Get Volume 2 @ 60strategies.com

www.ingramcontent.com/pod-product-compliance
Lightning Source LLC
Chambersburg PA
CBHW070253190526
45169CB00001B/391